AF600339

NATURAL LAW AND POSITIVE LAW

The writing of this dissertation was conducted under the direction of Dr. Stephan G. Kuttner, J.U.D., S.J.D., J.C.D., L.L.D., as major professor, and was approved by Rev. Clement V. Bastnagel, S.T.L., J.U.D., and Rev. John Rogg Schmidt, A.B., J.C.D., L.L.B., as readers.

THE CATHOLIC UNIVERSITY OF AMERICA
CANON LAW STUDIES
No. 393

NATURAL LAW AND POSITIVE LAW

A DISSERTATION

SUBMITTED TO THE FACULTY OF THE SCHOOL OF CANON LAW OF THE CATHOLIC UNIVERSITY OF AMERICA IN PARTIAL FULFILLMENT OF THE REQUIREMENTS FOR THE DEGREE OF DOCTOR OF CANON LAW

BY THE
REVEREND RAYMOND F. BÉGIN, A.B., S.T.L., J.C.L.
PRIEST OF THE DIOCESE OF PORTLAND

THE CATHOLIC UNIVERSITY OF AMERICA PRESS
WASHINGTON, D.C.
1959

NIHIL OBSTAT:

CLEMENT V. BASTNAGEL, S.T.L., J.U.D.
Censor Deputatus

Washingtonii, D.C., die 29 maii, 1958

IMPRIMATUR:

✠DANIEL J. FEENEY, *D.D.*
Episcopus Portlandensis

Portlandiae, die 31 maii, 1958

Printed by Theo. Gaus' Sons, Inc., Brooklyn 1, N. Y., U. S. A.

TO

MY MOTHER AND FATHER

AND

MANY BENEFACTORS

FOREWORD

Jurists are usually more immediately concerned with the technical elaboration and application of the laws which prevail in their own positive system. The difficulties inherent in such a task sometimes absorb their entire time and attention. This situation is somewhat deplorable. It is feared that an inferior knowledge of, or a lack of advertence to, the basic principles of law and justice may lead to a short-sighted view of the methods, tools and enactments of positive law.

In stressing the utility of the philosophy of law, the practical hegemony of the system in force is not overlooked. Nor is it asserted that a separate study of it is always indispensable to the lawyer. Through his native insight and good judgment, he may glean from the practice of law much of what he would normally learn from a theoretical investigation of its principles. For the solution of the more difficult problems, however, a deep understanding of the underlying theory of law is of invaluable assistance. Hence a great number of jurists have, through the ages, felt the need to deal with it explicitly.

In the present dissertation the writer studies the general relation of the positive systems of law to the nature of man and of human society, i.e., to the Natural Law. He thus hopes to contribute in some modest way to the modern revival of the theory of Natural Law as the foundation of law and justice. The limited scope of this work does not allow a historical investigation of the various schools of thought, past or present, which have dealt with these theoretical questions. No special attempt is made to trace to their original source the ideas accepted or rejected. After an introductory chapter on the notion of Right or Law in general, the two main chapters study in some detail the nature and function of the Natural Law and Positive Law respectively. Throughout these two chapters, the writer endeavors to show the necessary connections or relations between these two distinct but inseparable forms of Law. A final chapter serves as the general conclusion of the whole investigation, inasmuch as it indicates that most of the contrasts or conflicts of Positive Law with the Natural Law can be solved by a realistic approach to these problems.

The writer hereby expresses his gratitude to His Excellency, the Most Reverend Daniel J. Feeney, D.D., for the opportunity of graduate studies in Canon Law. He acknowledges very sincerely his deep indebtedness to Doctor Stephan Kuttner, for the invaluable assistance provided in the writing of this dissertation. He likewise thanks the Reverend Clement V. Bastnagel and the Reverend John Rogg Schmidt for having read the manuscript and offered judicious corrections. He does not wish to forget those kind friends whose constant encouragement served him in good stead in completing this work.

TABLE OF CONTENTS

CHAPTER II

CHAPTER III

CHAPTER IV

CHAPTER I

THE NATURE AND REGULATION OF RIGHT

Article I: The Definition of Right

Preliminary Remark

It will be useful to note immediately what the term *Right* is meant to signify in English in respect to the terms used in other languages. The Latin language has two words of closely related significance: *lex* and *ius*. The French similarly distinguish between *loi* and *droit*. The Italians differentiate likewise between the terms *legge* and *diritto*. The word *Right,* as it will be used throughout this dissertation, wants to convey the same idea as the terms *ius, droit* and *diritto*.[1]

SECTION 1.

COMMON CONCEPTION OF THE TERM RIGHT

While the etymological study of the term Right and its Latin counterpart *ius* would be most interesting, it is doubtful that it would lead to a clear philosophical definition.[2] Much is to be learned from the etymons of a word, but not the very essence of the thing it signifies.[3] Very often these root words reveal only the

---

[1] For purposes of clarity, the word *Right* will be capitalized whenever it is to signify the objective *ius, droit* and *diritto.*

[2] For a brief but penetrating study of the etymology of *ius,* see Graneris, *Philosophia Iuris,* Vol. I, *De Notione Iuris* (Torino: Società Editrice Internazionale; Romae: Libraria Pontificii Instituti Utriusque Iuris, 1943), pp. 31-37.

[3] ". . . aliud est etymologia nominis, et aliud est significatio nominis. Etymologia enim attenditur secundum *id a quo* imponitur nomen ad significandum; nominis vero significatio attenditur secundum *id ad quod* significandum nomen imponitur. Quare quandoque diversa sunt. . . ."—S. Thomas Aquinas, *Summa Theologiae,* cura et studio Instituti Studiorum Medievalium Ottaviensis ad textum S. Pii Papae V iussu confectum recognita, 2. ed., Commissio Piana, 5 vols. (Ottawa, Canada, 1953), IIaIIae, q. 92,a.1,ad 2um.

extrinsic notes or qualities attached to a thing: they fail to divulge its full and complete meaning as it is expressed in the derivative.[4] Let it suffice to say that from early Roman Law the term *ius*, translated into English by *Right*, denotes the object of justice, thus meaning that which is just, right or correct.[5]

In his search for a correct definition of Right, the philosopher begins with a confused idea taken from everyday experience. The chemist cannot attempt a scientific analysis of water before distinguishing between water and milk: this the common knowledge of men will teach him. So it is in the field of juridical phenomena, which comes under the scientific analysis of the philosopher.

It should not be surprising that the man on the street be somewhat cognizant of the meaning of Right. His whole life is indeed enmeshed in this reality. Forced by circumstances to live in society, he is well aware that there are some things he must do and others avoid. He fully realizes the practical meaning of Right when he says: I have the right to live in the house which I bought, and no one may stop me from doing so. True, he may not be able to give an exact definition of Right, but, if questioned properly,

---

[4] Bréal asserts: ". . . il n'est pas douteux que le langage désigne les choses d'une façon incomplète et inexacte. . . ." (p. 101) and later on (p. 102): "Les substantifs sont des signes attachés aux choses: ils renferment tout juste la part de vérité que peut renfermer un nom, part nécessairement d'autant plus petite que l'objet a plus de réalité."—*Essai de sémantique*, Paris, 1897; quoted by Graneris, who concludes: "Inde est quod ipsi moderni scientiae philologicae cultores caute nos monent nomina eorumve etymologias nunquam posse definitionem rerum exhibere, sed tantum indicia esse, ex quibus concludere valeamus, in rebus ipsis, tempore quo ita vocari coeperunt, agnitas fuisse notas iis vocibus expressas."—*Op. cit.*, I, 31.

[5] Ulpian says: "Iuri operam daturum prius nosse oportet, unde nomen iuris descendat. Est autem a iustitia appellatum: nam, ut eleganter Celsus definit, ius est ars boni et aequi. Cuius merito quis nos sacerdotes appellet: iustitiam namque colimus et boni et aequi notitiam profitemur, aequum ab iniquo separantes, licitum ab illicito discernentes. . . ."—*Corpus Iuris Civilis*, 3 vols., Vol. I, *Institutiones*, quas recognovit P. Krueger; *Digesta*, quae recognovit T. Mommsen et retractavit P. Krueger, ed. stereotypa 15.; Vol. II, *Codex Iustinianus*, quem recognovit et retractavit P. Krueger, ed. stereotypa 10.; Vol. III, *Novellae Constitutiones*, ed. stereotypa 5., a R. Schoell; opus Schoellii morte interceptum absolvit G. Kroll (Berolini: apud Weidmannos, 1928-1929), D. (1,1), 1, §2.

his answers would contain many valuable components of this definition.[6]

It will be useful to enumerate and analyze briefly the various characteristics of Right as furnished by the common knowledge of men.

a) Right belongs to the practical order, i.e. to the realm of human actions. Even a child will tell you that because this red and white bicycle is his, he may *do* something with it, whether it be to ride, paint or destroy it. He will also be convinced of his Right to resist the attempt on the part of his playmates to do the same without his permission.

b) Right is opposed to injury, as justice is to injustice, and pertains to the moral order.[6a] In every concrete case wherein a man professes to enjoy a Right to something, he maintains that it would be morally injurious to deprive him of this object.[7] He thus judges the morality of each act performed in regard to the thing over which he asserts a Right. It is morally correct and compulsory for others to respect this Right in their actions. To deprive him of it or to hinder him in the exercise of it is morally reprehensible.[8]

---

[6] Not every man is a philosopher of law, but men do act freely, i.e. deliberately. When a motorist drives carefully, he knows that he is not only protecting himself, but also respecting the Right of others to safe conduct on the highways. He recognizes what is Right in this instance. Similarly, not all legislators are students of law and its philosophy. Some of these, nevertheless, because of their native intelligence, are capable of discerning Right in its more common applications. It is in difficult and exceptional cases that a deeper insight into the nature of Right is indispensable to lawmakers. Briefly, one could say that there is some philosophy in every rational act, although it is not always conscious or reflective. See Bender, ***Philosophia Iuris*** (2. ed., Romae: Officium Libri Catholici, 1955), pp. 39-40. This work will be used extensively throughout this first chapter.

[6a] See *below*, pp. 38-39.

[7] There are limitations, of course, to the inviolability of the Rights of individuals, limitations imposed in view of the common good.

[8] The question of force or power does not enter into the common conception of Right. The poorest and weakest of men will contend that it is injurious for the rich to exploit his life and his health. Many a philosopher of Right by might would do well to consider the common estimation of humanity in this regard. It is difficult to understand how millions of men

c) The concept of Right implies the notion of sociability, i.e., it affects human acts in their connotation to other men. There is much difference between destroying a self-owned object,[8a] and burning down the house of a neighbor. The former action cannot be termed an injury because it does not concern anyone save the owner himself.[9] The latter, on the other hand, is a direct violation of Right, because it affects the lawful possession of another. In other words, one who has a Right to something is commonly admitted as having this Right in regard to somebody other than himself.

d) The idea of Right signifies something which is due to another as his own. When Peter asserts that Paul must pay the debt owed to him, he conveys more than the idea of a simple moral obligation. Paul is morally obliged to conserve his own life, and yet there is no question of Right here.[10] Only when Paul's action (in this case, the payment of a debt) is due to Peter as something belonging properly to him is the problem of Right involved.[11]

SECTION 2.

DEEPER INSIGHT INTO THE DEFINITION OF RIGHT

A. Terminology

In the preceding pages, it is easy to note that the substantive *right* has been used in two distinct but correlative meanings. Sen-

through the centuries should have been so wrong on such a fundamental point of the practical order.

[8a] Reference is intended to an object which has no other social implications, v.g., which is not insured.

[9] This does not mean that the action could not be morally wrong from another source. As it will be clearly shown below, Right is used here in the sense of justice, and deals with only that part of the moral order which regulates the actions of men in society as such. Because of the confusion which could result from an indiscriminate use of the words *right* and *wrong,* the present writer will endeavor to avoid using, without proper qualification, the term *wrong* to denote a social injury; similarly the term Right (capitalized) will designate only that which is morally correct in regard to other men in society.

[10] In the supposition that Paul's death or ill-health would not affect the Rights of others, v.g., his family.

[11] The four elements of Right explained above are taken from Bender, *Philosophia Iuris,* pp. 40-42.

tences like the following: "The concept of *Right* implies the notion of sociality," and "Peter has a *right* to enjoy his property," do not attach the same significance to the word *right*, although this distinction is not always clear in the minds of those who use this term. The first usage is in conformity with the first meaning given by Webster's Dictionary: "1. That which is right or correct. Specif.; a) Adherence to duty; obedience to lawful authority; freedom from guilt; specif., Ethics, that which is warranted by moral approval, the ideal of moral propriety. b) Just or righteous action or decision; justice; as, to petition as a matter of *right*."[12] A second meaning given by Webster is identical with the second sentence quoted above: "a power, privilege, or the like, vested in one by law.[13] It is not difficult to see immediately the relation between the two meanings. *Right* in the first sense is clearly the object of *right* in the second sense. It is almost tautological to say that one has the right to something because the object of his right is Right. The writer maintains that the first meaning of Right is fundamental,[14] and for that reason it alone will be studied *ex professo* in this search of a true definition.[15]

B. Difficulty in Giving a Definition of Right

To some philosophers of law, the exact definition of Right is most elusive and offers almost insuperable difficulties. Professor Giorgio del Vecchio says for instance:

> "Each of us knows approximately what Law is. The precise definition of the concept, however, presents notable difficulties. The proof one finds in the fact that the many researches carried out on this point have not yet led to results which

[12] *Webster's New Collegiate Dictionary*, 2. ed., Springfield, Mass.: G. & C. Merriam Co., 1956.

[13] *Loc. cit.*

[14] This will be stressed and explained more fully below. See corollary on Subjective Rights: their Meaning, pp. 15-16.

[15] The terms *ius, droit* and *diritto* are also used in three other senses: a) a law or collection of laws; b) the science of Right or Law; c) the legal order, either general or regarding a special field of social relations such as, v.g., the law of property (*ius proprietatis*). The writer will abstract from these three meanings here.

are universally accepted. 'The jurists are still seeking for a definition of their concept of Law,' said Emmanuel Kant; and these words have not perhaps, even today, lost their force entirely." [16]

The difficulties in arriving at a common definition of Right should perhaps be traced to the philosophical systems which many authors embrace rather than to the enigma of Right itself. Del Vecchio asserts:

> "If . . . we look to History the answer cannot be univocal, because History will answer by describing the manifold variety of ordinances and juridical institutes which have existed among the different peoples in their successive stages. Every people at every period determines in its own way what is Law." [17]

The last sentence in this quotation should be challenged if it really means what it says. The people of every age do not determine what is Law or Right, but rather they enact laws which determine what Rights the citizens will enjoy. In other words, the concept of Law or Right is not changed by the vicissitudes of juridical institutes. Right is Right and its notion must be abstracted from the constant and essential elements which the philosopher draws from experience. The lack of agreement on the notion of Right stems from Kantian preconceived ideas to which reality must conform. In this manner of thinking, it is no wonder that there are "*tot sensus quot capita.*" [18]

---

[16] *Philosophy of Law* (trans. from 8. ed. by Thomas Owen Martin, Washington, D.C.: The Catholic University of America Press, 1953), p. 244. One should note that the Italian word *diritto* is translated by Law (capitalized). With due respect to his learned professor, the writer prefers to translate it by *Right,* in order to distinguish it from a law considered as the enactment of a superior.

[17] *Op. cit.,* pp. 244-245.

[18] "Haec assertio [i.e., that of Del Vecchio quoted above] gravem manifestat errorem circa modum quo philosophus interrogare debet historiam seu rerum naturam. Eundem errorem committerem dicens: inutile est interrogare historiam vel naturam ut sciam quid sit animal, nam in historia et in rerum natura invenimus multa et diversa animalia et non

C. In Search of a True Definition

1. Right is a Relation

One of the essential elements of Right already acquired from the common knowledge of men is that of sociability.[19] It is impossible to conceive of Right without taking into consideration at least two persons. To say merely that a person has a Right is to form an incomplete sentence. The question which always comes to mind is: a Right to what? or a Right toward whom? This observation helps to classify Right in its proper category of being.

Among the perfections of man there are some that are absolutely essential to his being, such as rationality and animality, and others which are non-essential and therefore are called accidental. The latter in turn are either absolute or relative. Absolute perfections are so called because they complement an individual considered in respect to himself alone; beauty and slenderness are of this sort, and fall under the categories of quality and quantity respectively. Relative perfections, on the other hand, cannot be understood as the attributes of a subject except in regard to another person or thing. These are classified under the category of relation.

Maternity is a clear example of a relative perfection. It is a very real perfection, existing in each mother: the physical, psychological and spiritual transformation which takes place in a woman through motherhood is sufficient foundation for a real relation. And yet one cannot qualify her as a mother without at least implicit reference to her child, which is the term of this relation of maternity. So also the perfection ascribed to a person as the possessor of a Right is a relative perfection, a relation. The next point of investigation will be to consider the term or object of this relation.

---

ipsum animal. Philosophus cum fructu interrogare potest historiam, sed ea conditione ut recte interroget, i.e. ut interroget tamquam philosophus et non tamquam historicus; et responsione accepta cum ea agat tamquam philosophus et non tamquam historicus. Non enim agitur de cognoscendo facta, sed de *cognoscendo ea, quae facta nos docent in materia philosophica.* Etiam bene interrogare est ars, qua non omnes pollent."—Bender, *Philosophia Iuris,* p. 46, note. (Italics are the writer's).

[19] See *above,* p. 6.

2. The Term or Object of Right is the Action or Omission of Others[20]

It may seem strange, at first sight, to assert that the term of Right is the action or omission of others. When a proprietor says that he has a Right to his house, it appears that the house itself is the object of his Right. There are, however, certain Rights which manifestly have no material thing as their object, such as, for instance, the Right to walk, to sing and to speak. In order to resolve this problem adequately, it will be necessary to outline a few fundamental notions of the juridical order.

It has already been established that Right pertains to the practical order of human activity. It is a basic thesis of philosophy that whatever man does he does for a purpose, an end which he chooses.[21] Desiring this end, he will act to obtain it, using the necessary means. These actions may be distinguished into two categories. The first comprises those actions in which man does not make use of exterior things, for example, to sing or to talk. Here it is evident that the sole means of attaining the end in question, v.g., fame, is the action of man, the exercise of his faculties. Much more frequent, however, are those actions which require the use of exterior things, such as eating bread. But there again careful attention reveals that the means to the end, v.g., the sustenance of life, is immediately and directly the *action* of eating, and only mediately or indirectly the object called bread.

When one considers man in society, as living in a community with other human beings, the same considerations come into play. In order to develop the full potentialities of his nature, man needs the help of others.[22] If he is to achieve peace and happiness, which

---

[20] Here again the writer follows closely the explanations of Bender, *Philosophia Iuris*, pp. 47 60.

[21] It is impossible to study in detail all the fundamental notions of moral philosophy. Some things have to be presupposed. Briefly, it may be useful to point out that the will is the prime mover in man; for this faculty determines man to certain actions because it is attracted by the goodness of the purpose or the end to which these actions lead. Desire for good (real or apparent) rules man.

[22] The social nature of man is another fundamental moral thesis which is presupposed here, although it will be studied in some detail later on.

is the end and purpose of society, his own actions will not suffice: he must have the co-*operation* of his fellowmen. This co-operation takes on two aspects: negative and positive. For example, if Peter is to preserve his life, he relies upon the fact that his neighbors will not kill him or will not destroy his crop of wheat or his cattle (negative aspect: omission). He also depends on their collaboration in supplying a police force to protect his life and that of others, in selling him grain for his cattle and fertilizer for his crop (positive aspect: action). Thus for every necessity of his life, Peter will have the Right to demand the co-operation of others. Properly considered then, the term or object of Right as a relation is the *action* or *omission* of others.

This being true, how is it possible to legitimize such assertions as: Peter has the Right to his house? In this common mode of expression, the object of Peter's Right seems to be a thing. A closer examination reveals that the phrase is but an abbreviated manner of describing the full reality. Inasmuch as it is impossible to enumerate in a detailed manner all the possible actions open to Peter in regard to his house, one says simply that he has a Right to his house.[23]

There is another difficulty suggested by common usage. If it is correct to say that Peter has a Right to his house, where do the actions or omissions of others come in? Are they not supposed to be the term or the object of Right? The answer is again found in the abbreviated manner of everyday speech. The full statement should read: Peter has a Right that others place no obstacle to his use of the house he possesses. If no other persons save Peter were involved, there would be no Right at all. Peter would simply make use of his house without any thought of having the right to do so.[24]

---

[23] The permissible actions in regard to a Right are determined by the law which grants that Right. See Article 4 of this chapter: Laws as Norms of Right, pp. 31-40.

[24] For a philosophical analysis of the various modes of expressing a Right, see Bender, *Philosophia Iuris*, pp. 51-56.

3. The Necessity Implied in Right is Taken from Man's Purpose in Life[25]

The concept of Right contains the important element of necessity: it suggests that something is due to someone.[26] The basis of this necessity is teleological: it is founded in the exigencies of the common good of humanity. All men tend toward a goal of perfect peace and happiness. Unlike plants who are subordinated to animals as the latter are to men, man is not subordinated to any other creature in this world. He has an end unto himself: his own personal development or perfection, i.e., happiness.[27] Although man enjoys free will, he cannot escape this moral ordination to his ultimate end.[28]

It is inconceivable that man should be directed necessarily toward a goal without at the same time being obliged to utilize the necessary means leading to that goal. If Peter must go to Churchill Lake and the only way to reach this destination is by airplane, he must fly. As explained above, the primary means of man's perfection are his actions, and, because of his social nature, the actions or omissions of his fellowmen. Whenever there exists a

---

[25] In this matter, besides Bender, *op. cit.*, pp. 60-63, see Lachance, *Le Concept de Droit selon Aristote et S. Thomas* (Montréal: éd. Albert Levesque; Paris: Recueil Sirey, 1933), pp. 257-268; and also Funk, *De Jure Naturali Transcendente Jus Positivum* (Romae: Pontificia Universitas Gregoriana, 1947), pp. 84-89.

[26] According to Wolff, this element is implied in the Roman concept of *Ius*. "*Ius*, it seems to the reviewer, is all that a person—whether in a private or in a public capacity—or a group does or claims by way of exercising a power, provided this power is acknowledged (not granted!) and protected by the gods or, later, under a rationally conceived legal order, by the magistrate of the Roman people."—"Notes and Reviews," Review of *Das altrömische Ius*, Studien zur Rechtsgeschichte and Rechtsvorstellung der Römer (von Max Kaser), *Seminar, Annual Extraordinary Number of The Jurist* (Washington, D.C.: The Catholic University of America Canon Law School), VII (1949), 91.

[27] This may seem to be a selfish viewpoint, but it is perfectly legitimate. Man cannot deny his innate desire for perfection: it is stronger than himself.

[28] Man's free will entitles him to choose between this and that good, but never allows him to go outside the realm of good, either real or apparent. Otherwise one could come to the contradictory conclusion that man wants and does not want happiness at one and the same time.

necessary link between the actions (omissions) of others and a person's goal of happiness, there is established a relation of Right between this person and the actions (omissions) of others.[29] The field of Right, then, is much restricted by this element of necessity included in it.[30]

These considerations lead to the conclusion that the relation of Right establishes that whatever is due to a person is due to him in such a strict manner that it is already his own. If Peter, for example, has lent an automobile to Paul, the relation of Right existing between Peter and the restoration by Paul is such that the automobile which is to be restored, although it might be in the possession of Paul, is truly Peter's own automobile.[31]

4. Right Is a Relation Founded on the Equality of Men

All men are equal in regard to their ultimate goal. Participating in the same rational nature, they all tend toward happiness. Because of this fundamental equality, they must all share in the use of the means necessary to the fulfillment of their desire for happiness. Equality is not Right, but it is the cause of Right.[32]

---

[29] It should be noted immediately that, because of the closely-knit ties existing between men in society, the means to his goal which every man has a right to expect and demand are dependent upon the common good. The Rights of one man are therefore limited by those of others.

[30] There are many corollaries to be drawn from this point. The juridical order is concerned only with the fundamentals and essentials of social life: "De minimis non curat praetor." The field of Right or Law is therefore minimized in some way. The need is felt, consequently, for other elements of conduct to enter the social picture, such as the precept of charity promulgated by Christ. There are bound to be many *lacunae* in a system of life which is based solely upon juridical necessity and where every man insists at all times upon the full respect of his Rights. The virtue of magnanimity, for instance, would do much more to relieve tension and discord than the constant insistence upon one's Rights. See Funk, *op. cit.*, pp. 87-88.

[31] The same observation cannot be made in regard to the things demanded simply by utility or convenience. A greeting or a gesture of politeness may be due to a person, but certainly not in the same strict manner as an automobile belonging to him.

[32] "Haec aequalitas non est ius. Nam haec aequalitas est relatio inter *hominem* et *hominem*. Ius non est relatio inter hominem et hominem, sed

When speaking of the equality of men, one must not interpret it mathematically. The similitude among men begins and ends in their rational nature. The different modes of equality are determined by the conditions and circumstances in which men are born and live. It is pure fantasy to conceive of a world in which all men would be equal in status and manner of living. The existence of any order supposes that functions will be distributed according to the needs of this order and the aptitudes of the individuals involved.[33] There will always be a distinction between laborers and executives, between rulers and subjects, between Popes and priests. If there is to be an equality of Right among men, it can only be a proportionate one. Each man is to have whatever is necessary for his own happiness, but since conditions and circumstances differ from man to man, one will require more than the other.[34] Under this proper conception of Right, all men remain equal, because they individually have all that they need for their individual happiness.[35]

D. Conclusion

The definition of Right which flows from the analysis of its various elements can now be given. Right is the relation existing between one person and the action or omission of another, accord-

---

inter hominem et *rem,* sicut supra explicatum est. Tamen haec aequalitas intime connexa est cum iure. Ius causatur ab hac aequalitate in ordine causalitatis finalis. Est enim ista aequalitas finis iuris. Ius existit, ut homines sint aequales seu ut quilibet habeat necessaria ad finem proprium consequendum."—Bender, *Philosophia Iuris,* p. 64. (Italics are the author's).

[33] Compare with St. Paul's first Epistle to the Corinthians, XII, 4-12.

[34] The term *equality,* although commonly used by philosophers and jurists, is therefore somewhat misleading. It is to be understood in only a very relative sense. The notion of equality is analogical: it applies more readily to mathematical equations than to proportionate distributions.

[35] This is the philosophical ideal, which, as experience teaches us, is very hard to attain. On this earth one must be content with approximative equality. Laws (which are the norms of Right) require careful planning. Despite the honest and sincere efforts of legislators, their wisdom is only finite and therefore incapable of meeting and satisfying the constant changes of human life and activity. Imperfect laws are, however, better than none, and if they are obeyed scrupulously they will certainly enhance the cause of justice in the social order. Cf. Bender, *op. cit.,* pp. 66-67.

ing to which this person may demand this action or omission as due to him on the strength of the equality of men, in virtue of the common good, goal of happiness toward which all men strive.[36]

E. Corollary: Subjective Rights: their Meaning

If there is one characteristic that stands out in the definition of Right given above, then that is its objectivity. The determinant factors in the circumscription of Right are the common good of humanity and the means necessary for each individual to attain it. These factors are evaluated by reason and thus give birth to a "concretization" of Right expressed in laws. Right, as a concept, has no real existence except in the subjects of whom it is predicated.

When the English language uses expressions such as "Peter has the right to use his house," it conveys the idea, not altogether correct philosophically, that Peter is endowed with a special faculty or power whereby he is free to act as he pleases in regard to his own house.[37] Similarly, many modern philosophers define Right principally in terms of a moral power or faculty over one's own thing: in this they are the followers of Suarez (1548-1617).[38] The fallacy contained in the English expression and in the definitions of these authors is the confusion between the Right and the permission or possibility of the exercise thereof. It is perfectly legitimate for English-speaking people to use similar phrases, provided they are properly understood. So also is it feasible to divide Right into objective and subjective, and to describe the latter as a moral power or faculty of the will.[39] It is not correct to say, however,

[36] Bender, *op. cit.,* p. 67.

[37] This is indeed the second meaning of Right given by Webster. Cf. *above,* p. 7.

[38] "Et juxta posteriorem et *strictam* juris significationem solet *proprie* jus vocari facultas quaedam moralis, quam unusquisque habet circa rem suam, vel ad rem sibi debitam."—*Opera Omnia,* ed. nova a Carolo Breton, Vols. V and VI: *Tractatus de Legibus et Legislatore Deo* (Parisiis, 1856), L. I., c.2,n.4; (hereafter cited *De Legibus*). Bender, (*op. cit.,* pp. 69, 70 nn. 4 and 5) gives a list of authors who define Right in the same manner.

[39] Bender frowns on the use of the term *moral faculty* by philosophers. "Si quis hanc licentiam agendi vocari velit facultatem moralem, imponit

that the primary significance of Right is a moral faculty. To say that a person has the right to his house is to assert in reality that there is a relation of necessity between this person and the actions (omissions) of others in regard to that house, and that, in accordance with this Right as already objectively existing, this person may lawfully use his house in whatever way he chooses,[40] without fear of disturbance on the part of others. It is in that sense, and in that sense alone, that one can speak of subjective rights.[41]

The foregoing discussion was not meant to be purely academic; it was meant to emphasize that Right is not ultimately founded on the will of man, on human liberty. To define Right as the moral faculty of the will and to assign liberty as its end is, in fact, to presuppose that the dictate of the will is the rule of morality and the foundation of Justice. The door is thus open to the aberrations and vagaries of tyrants who will not be governed by reason and by the common good of humanity.[42]

Article II: The Subject of Right

It is clear that a Right which belongs to nobody in particular is no Right at all. The relation of Right (objective meaning of Right) has its foundation in a subject (subjective meaning of Right), i.e., in one who is lawfully enabled to act or refrain from acting, and who may enjoin others to act or refrain from acting

---

alicui rei nomen, detorquens illud ad sensum omnino improprium."—*Philosophia Iuris,* p. 77.

[40] Again within the limits imposed by the common good and the individual Rights of others.

[41] It is by virtue of analogy that subjective rights take the name of Right, i.e., because of their close connection with it. As St. Thomas (1225-1274) stated: "illud quod est propter se est prius eo quod est propter aliud." —*Summa Theologiae,* Ia, q.6,a.2; q.13,a.6; a.15,a.1,ad 3um. Objective Right is certainly primary in regard to subjective right, which is but the lawful possibility of the exercise thereof. On this whole question of moral faculty and subjective right, see Lachance, *Le Concept de Droit selon Aristote et S. Thomas,* pp. 397-417.

[42] See Lachance, *op. cit.,* pp. 401-402. This point will be studied in detail in the later treatment of laws which are the norms of Right.

in compliance with this Right.[43] The purpose of this article is to determine the proper subjects of Right.

SECTION 1.

ALL PERSONS ARE SUBJECTS OF RIGHT

In the preceding article, it was explained that the concept of Right is essentially teleological. It presupposes the existence of a subject endowed in some way with an intellectual nature which renders him capable of willing his end and using the means to attain it. The term normally reserved to designate an individual possessing such characteristics is that of *person.*[44]

To attribute personality to a being is to assert its superiority over the other creatures of this world. A person is an intelligent and free being, the master of its actions and its destiny, and open to a whole new world of knowledge and love unknown to purely material beings. Maritain aptly states:

> "Such a being must exist not only as other things do, but eminently, in self-possession, holding itself in hand, master of itself. In short, it must be endowed with a spiritual existence, capable of containing itself thanks to the operations of the intellect and freedom, capable of super-existing by way of knowledge and of love. For this reason, the metaphysical tradition of the West defines the person in terms of independence, as a reality which, subsisting spiritually, constitutes a universe unto itself, a relatively independent whole within

[43] "Il va sans dire qu'un droit qui n'appartient à personne n'est pas un droit. L'idée de droit implique précisément une possession en propre, une aliénation du pouvoir des autres à en jouir au même titre que soi. Si toutes choses sont dûes à tous et à personne, il n'y a plus de droits, mais une liberté sans ordre. Il faut donc qu'il y ait quelque détenteur du droit." —Lachance, *Le Concept de Droit selon Aristote et Saint Thomas,* p. 333.

[44] It is outside the scope of this dissertation to attempt a thorough study of the metaphysical notion of personality. One could consult the long treatise on this matter by Garrigou-Lagrange in *Christ the Savior,* trans. by Dom Bede Rose (St. Louis and London: B. Berder Book Co., 1950), 119-172; and Maritain, *Les Degrés du Savoir* (5.ed., Paris: Desclée & Co., 1946), 845-853. It will suffice here to outline certain points which affect the juridical order more directly.

the great whole of the universe, facing the transcendent whole which is God." [45]

The concept of personality implies much more than that of individuation (in philosophical language). By virtue of its individuation, a material being becomes autonomous, i.e., it acquires a subsistence distinct and independent from that of other beings. Under the various accidental transformations which it undergoes, the individual subject remains the same, undivided in itself and separable from others.[46] Over and above individuation, the notion of personality adds to a subject the characteristics of a rational nature, featuring the spiritual operations of the intellect and the will.[47] Endowed with intelligence, a person is able to reflect upon himself, his thoughts and actions,[48] to take cognizance of his

[45] *The Person and the Common Good* (London: Geoffrey Bles, 1948), 28-29.

[46] Thomistic philosophers commonly teach that the principle of individuation is matter connoting a certain quantity, according to which a subject occupies in space a position distinct from every other position. "Illa quae differunt numero in genere substantiae, non solum differunt accidentibus, sed etiam forma et materia. Sed si quaeratur, quare haec forma differt ab illa, non erit alia ratio, nisi quia est in alia materia signata. Nec invenitur alia ratio, quare haec materia sit divisa ab illa, nisi propter quantitatem. Et ideo materia subjecta dimensioni intelligitur esse principium hujus diversitatis."—S. Thomas, *Expositio Super Librum Boethii De Trinitate,* ed. B. Decker (Leiden: Brill, 1955), q.4,a.2, ad 4um. For a more complete study of the principle of individuation, see Gredt, *Elementa Philosophiae Aristotelico-Thomisticae* (7. ed., 2 vols., Friburgi Brisgoviae: B. Herder & Co., 1937), I, 295-304.

[47] In a human being the two metaphysical aspects of individuation and personality "are not two separate things. There is not in me one reality, called my individual, and another reality, called my person. One and the same reality is, in a certain sense, an individual, and, in another sense, a person. Our whole being is an individual by reason of that in us which derives from matter, and a person by reason of that in us which derives from spirit."—Maritain, *The Person and the Common Good,* pp. 30-31.

[48] "Come si vede, c'è un abisso tra questa concezione et quella della filosofia moderna. Non si può ridurre la persona alla coscienza, poichè la persona è un *prius,* in confronto alla coscienza. Ho coscienza di me e di quanto avviene in me, perchè sono persona, non viceversa. La coscienza di qualcosa e la consapevolezza di sè testificano e mi rivelano la natura del mio io; ma non sono il mio io, bensì lo presuppongono."—Olgiati, *Il*

needs, to formulate the ideal which corresponds to his aspirations, to judge the value of his acts in relation to a definite purpose. As a result of the freedom of his will, a person acquires a certain mastery over his actions. Unlike non-rational beings, he rises above the blind forces of determinism and assumes responsibility for his conduct.[49] For those reasons, St. Thomas says that subjects enjoying intelligence and free will deserve the special name of persons.[50]

It is easy to conclude, then, that all persons, and only persons, are the proper subjects of Right. This is due, in short, to their capacity of pursuing an end of their own by the judicious selection of the means necessary for this purpose.

SECTION 2. ALL MEN ARE SUBJECTS OF RIGHT

The term *person* is analogous, i.e., it may be applied to or predicated of various beings, but with notable differences. The first application is to physical persons, in opposition to moral persons. One could say that the essential distinction between a physical and a moral person lies in the principle of unity of the being under consideration. If the principle of unity is substantial, i.e., concrete, the person is physical; if the principle of unity is not substantial but accidental, i.e., pertaining to the order of finality, there results a moral union and therefore a moral person.[51]

Concetto di Giuridicità in San Tommaso D'Aquino (2.ed., Milano: Società Editrice "Vita E Pensiero," 1944), p. 100.

[49] Only the reader who accepts the doctrine of the spirituality of man will admit these developments. The writer does not lose sight of the great influence of environment and circumstances in the shaping of a person's life. He does, however, believe that the postulate of moral responsibility is the only stable foundation for a sound juridical order.

[50] "Inter ceteras substantias quoddam speciale nomen habent singularia rationalis naturae. Et hoc nomen est persona."—*Summa Theologiae,* Ia,q.29, a.1.—The difference between individual and person is admirably well treated in Lachance, *op. cit.,* pp. 334-342.

[51] The problem of moral persons as subjects of Right will be studied in the following section.

The characteristics of a person are eminently united in man.[52] Del Vecchio says:

> "If we recall that Law refers essentially to will and to operation, we can readily understand that only those can be subjects of Law[53] who have naturally the capacity to will and to operate. These essential psychological requisites are found above all in man. He has within himself the natural conditions for regulating his own activity. He is capable of imposing upon himself and upon others a direction and a limit of operation. He can demand, put forth a right to a certain behavior from others, and can recognize himself, in turn, as subject to an obligation. We can, therefore, assert the maxim that *every man is a subject of Law,* insofar as he has naturally a capacity to will and to determine himself with regard to others." [54]

As Del Vecchio himself admits, this principle was not always accepted throughout the course of history. One recalls the inferior treatment given to slaves and foreigners in early Roman Law. It is significant to note, however, that progress in civilization, accentuated by the influence of Christianity, has considerably strengthened the principle that all human beings, regardless of status or condition, are the subjects of Right.[55]

It is impossible to emphasize too strenuously the principle enunciated above. By the very fact that a man is a man, a rational creature, he is the subject of Right.[56] The proponents of euthanasia

---

[52] To say that man's personality is superior to that of moral persons does not deny the infinite transcendence of this perfection in God. As the Creator of mankind, God's Rights (if we may speak of Rights in God) are to be asserted over those of all others. If properly respected, these Rights serve as the true guide for the correct appreciation of the dignity of the human person, created in the image of God. The greatness of man is due to his resemblance, however remote, to his Master.

[53] I.e., Right. See note 16, p. 8.

[54] *Philosophy of Law,* p. 338.

[55] Even in Roman times, the harshness of slavery was mitigated, v.g., by the *"ius peculii"* and by protection against unreasonably cruel masters. Foreigners, similarly, were treated quite equitably under the *"ius gentium."*

[56] To speak of animals as having Rights is to speak very improperly.

would do well to analyze this statement carefully. A genius has no more the Right to live than a newly-born infant whose intellectual faculties are not at all developed as yet. The presence of physical or psychic obstacles to the proper exercise of a man's rationality does not for one minute do away with his rational nature. It would be theoretically and practically absurd to maintain that the criterion of man's Rights is his ability to act as a fully rational being at all times. The principles of Right, like all other principles of being, are established according to essentials, i.e., upon the essential nature of man, and not upon some fortuitous accident which allows him (or not) to exercise his manhood.[57]

The same observations apply to the unborn human fetus. Birth, as well as the circumstances in which the fetus evolves, are things accidental: they do not change the nature of the being which is brought forth into the world. If, as modern science professes, the newly-conceived fetus has a life of its own, which is entirely distinct from that of the mother, and if after some months it is to emerge as a human baby, the logical conclusion is that it is already a distinct human being in the womb of the mother: it is therefore a subject of Right.

It should be remembered that the present discussion on the subject of Right does not deal specifically with positive legislation on the part of the various States. The latter, in general, do not attribute Rights to unborn fetuses. This is a practical rule that may seem necessary for the proper order of positive law. In theory it is an erroneous attitude and could lead to very injurious results if certain corrective measures were not applied. The unborn fetus, for example, has the Right of succession as regards

---

Their existence is conditioned by their usefulness to men. The latter, however, in response to their own rational nature must not abuse them. See Bender, *Philosophia Iuris*, pp. 91-95.

[57] No one would dare assert that whenever a man does not act in a specifically rational manner, v.g., in sleep or in a drunken stupor, he thereby loses his human Rights. Regardless of how insane a person is, he remains a human being and must be treated as such; it is only by virtue of some organic or functional disease that he is unable to respond normally. Scientists will nevertheless agree that there is an immense difference between a completely insane person and an animal.

the father who dies before the mother delivers the child: this Right is usually sanctioned by positive law, thus forming a tacit admission that a fetus is, in fact, the subject of Right.[58]

SECTION 3.

MORAL PERSONS AS SUBJECTS OF RIGHT[59]

The existence of moral persons is founded upon the social nature of man. His objective needs and purposes are so complex and his subjective means so inadequate, that the individual alone cannot prove sufficient to his task. He must associate with others and form organizations dedicated to the attainment of the particular ends in view. These collective entities have a being of their own, distinct from that of their members. True, they have no physical being, but they do exist and operate in fact, through the members who serve as their agents.

Many are the theories concerning the precise nature of these entities. The better view seems to be expressed by Del Vecchio:

> "The juridical persons . . . have a reality, be it *sui generis*, that is, not sensible, but intelligible, as the realities of Law precisely are. There exists always a natural basis, an ensemble of effective and concrete needs upon which the entity is founded. This is a living force, exercising real, actual, functions."[60]

Although they do not exist except in the individuals and do not operate except through the actions of these individuals, these entities have an essentially social being and activity. They are created by the co-ordination of willing and operating between individuals striving towards a common purpose, and are, therefore, properly

[58] Already one sees the possibility of conflict between the natural law and the positive law. This problem is treated specifically in Chapters III and IV. Concerning the fetus as subject of Right, see Bender, *Philosophia Iuris*, pp. 86-91.

[59] Canon Law uses the term *moral person*, which corresponds to what the civil jurists call a *juridical person*.

[60] *Philosophy of Law*, p. 344.—To discuss all the theories expounded by philosophers and jurists on this point seems unnecessary in this dissertation.

moral persons.[61] The moral order is, indeed, an order of finality.[62]

A perfect example of a moral person as a subject of Right is the State. It exists in the society of its individual members, but independently of this or that one. They come and go, and the State remains. Its objectives, summed up in the notion of the common good, do not necessarily coincide with the good of individuals taken separately. Its rules and laws are enforced by an authority superior to that of its several constituents. Each State is autonomous, distinct and separate from all others. In brief, it is a person, and therefore the subject of Right.[63]

So far, attention has been focused on those moral or juridical persons which come under the category of corporations. As a matter of fact, it is the only form of juridical persons recognized in classical Roman Law.[64] There are, however, other moral persons, known under the name of foundations or institutes, which are construed in various systems as corporations sole or "goods

---

[61] For that reason it seems preferable to call them moral persons, and not merely juridical persons.

[62] "La personne morale est essentiellement constituée par la volonté collective des individus qui forment la société, c'est-à-dire par *l'accord des volontés individuelles considérées comme un tout.* Lorsqu'on oppose la société aux individus, on entend par *société l'ensemble des individus, en tant que réalisant une oeuvre commune,* et par *individus, les hommes* considérés isolément *en tant que chacun recherche son bien propre.* Il s'agit donc toujours des hommes et rien que des hommes mais sous deux aspects différents de leur activité."—Leclercq, *Leçons de droit naturel* (4 vols. in 5, Vol. I: *Le fondement du droit et de la société,* 3.éd., 1948, Vol. II: *L'Etat ou la politique,* 3.éd., 1948, Vol. III: *La famille,* 2.éd., 1945, Vol. IV: *Les droits et devoirs individuels,* P.I.: *Vie, disposition de soi,* 2.éd., 1946, P.II. *Travail, propriété,* 2.éd., 1946 (Namur: Ad. Wesmael-Charlier; Louvain: Société D'Etudes Morales, Sociales et Juridiques), I, 318; italics are the author's. See also Messner, *Social Ethics,* trans. by J. J. Doherty (St. Louis & London: B. Herder Book Co., 1949), pp. 116-117.

[63] These properties of a person, attributable by analogy to the State, are well described by Lachance, *Le Concept de Droit . . . ,* pp. 367-369.

[64] The opportunity is here offered to point out that moral persons are not created by the State. How, otherwise, would the State come into existence? For reasons of the common good and security, the State may and does regulate them, giving them an official status before the positive law.

dedicated by an irrevocable act of the will to a certain purpose, customarily with a character of perpetuity or of indefinite duration." [65] How can one use the term *person* to designate such inanimate entities? For many authors it should be understood only in a most improper sense, since these moral persons are but fictions of law.[66] Del Vecchio believes that, although the real element is more apparent here, foundations still deserve the name of persons because of the pervading will of the founder which is objective and irrevocable.[67] Perhaps the more acceptable solution lies in considering as the subjects of Right in these cases the men by whom and for whose benefit the property is administered, whether they be determined or not. In that sense these foundations can be considered as true and not only metaphorical persons.[68]

Article III: The Coercibility of Right

SECTION 1.
NATURE OF COERCIBILITY

After the explanations presented in the two previous articles, the coercibility of Right should offer no serious difficulties. The attribution of a Right to a subject is the equivalent of asserting that this person may lawfully demand that all others respect this Right. Whenever this respect is accorded to the possessor of a Right, he need not go any further: he simply exercises it in the peaceful tranquillity of the social order. But inasmuch as this is not always the case, the subject of a Right is empowered, either by himself or through society,[69] to use whatever means necessary, even physical, to protect his Right. While it is true that might does not make Right, there is a certain power or force attached to Right, as there is a certain force or potentiality implied in the

---

[65] Del Vecchio, *Philosophy of Law,* p. 346.

[66] Bender (*op. cit.,* p. 100) compares the legislator to the technician who uses negative and imaginary quantities to make his computations of reality. Lachance (*op. cit.,* p. 357) holds a similar opinion.

[67] *Op. cit.,* p. 346.

[68] Graneris, *Philosophia Iuris,* p. 76.

[69] See *below,* p. 29ff.

perfection of any being.[70] There would be no value to a Right which was not strong, i.e., which could not be enforced physically, if need be, upon its proposed violators. This, in general, is the meaning of the coercibility of Right.

For a deeper insight into this question, the coercibility of Right may be defined as the Right which the possessor of a certain Right or society has, namely to use physical force in order to see this certain Right prevail.[71] There are two Rights involved in this definition. The first, which may be called primary, is the one which requires protection, for example, the Right to live. The second, called secondary, necessarily flows from the primary Right in order to offer this protection. If the Right to live has any consistency and any real meaning, it must logically entail the Right to use force against aggressors. It is in that sense that one may attribute coercibility to the Right to live.[72]

Coercibility must be carefully distinguished from coaction. The latter implies the actual use of force, to which the possessor is not always obliged or entitled to have recourse. In a normal state of affairs, such action will prove unnecessary for the proper enjoyment of a Right. It may happen, furthermore, that a person

[70] "Se ci liberiamo dal senso di repulsione che una parola simile—la forza—per uno scherzo dell'immaginazione e per l'imprecisione del linguaggio provoca in noi; se analizziamo razionalmente il fatto, o i fatti, che ci manifestano la forza, per elaborare anche queste esperienze in funzione del concetto di ente, subito vediamo che 'forza' significa la potentialità di un essere e si riduce, quindi, al concetto di essere e di perfezione. Tale potenza potrà essere bene o male usata; ma non si può confondere il cattivo uso d'una realtà con la realtà in sè stessa, tanto che essa potrebbe venir utilizzata in modo contrario."—Olgiati, *Il Concetto di Giuridicità in San Tommaso d'Aquino*, p. 194.

[71] Cf. Bender, *Philosophia Iuris*, p. 125; Del Vecchio, *Philosophy of Law*, p. 297.

[72] Such is the explanation of Bender, *loc. cit.* While the writer accepts the general notion of coercibility given by Bender, he wishes to point out that coercibility is not a Right in itself, i.e., not a primary Right, and therefore not coercible (*ad infinitum*). Perhaps it would be better to speak of the "permissibility" or "lawfulness" of using coercion, as a result of the possession of a Right. Possible confusion would thus be avoided, and the nature of coercibility, a consequence of every primary Right, would still be well defined.

may not have the necessary means of coaction. Does this mean that he thereby loses his Rights? Not at all. Only those who confuse coaction (exercise of physical power) with coercibility (moral and juridical *Right* to use power) would proffer such a statement. The door would thus be opened wide to the Right of the stronger. The man who commands an army, on the contrary, has no more the Right to use force to protect his life than the poor beggar who is assailed by maniacs on the street. Circumstances may prevent the beggar from being physically able to protect this Right; they do not rob him of it.[73]

A well-established distinction between coercibility and coaction answers very well the objection of some authors who contend that force is not essential to Right or to Law.[74] According to them, the respect of a person's Right is ordinarily spontaneous, due to psychological motives independent of physical force. As a matter of fact, the existence of a social order founded solely upon force would be utterly impossible. Only in exceptional cases (providing, therefore, no basis for a general rule) is coaction necessary. It is hoped, furthermore, that in a more perfect society, one enhanced by a higher regard for moral values, the necessity of recourse to physical constraint will have practically vanished. Will, then, Right cease to exist, for the absence of coaction?[75]

Besides seeming somewhat utopian in its conception of society on this earth, the views expressed in this objection do not contradict the thesis of the coercibility of Right.[76] Given a situation or

[73] This is the explanation of Bender, *op. cit.*, pp. 126-128. The author also points out that the use of force must be proportionate, insofar as possible, to the past or proposed violation. *Ibid.*, p. 129, n.2.

[74] The writer agrees that neither coercibility nor coaction are of the essence of Right, but affirms that coercibility is a natural consequence of Right, whose existence is already presupposed. It is a quality which flows from the essence already constituted.

[75] This objection is ascribed to F. Trendelenburg (1802-1872) and H. Ahrens (1808-1874) by Del Vecchio, *Philosophy of Law*, p. 298.

[76] A Christian finds it difficult to conciliate this optimistic sentiment with the doctrine of the original downfall of man and the evident fact of man's evil tendencies. A realistic non-believer, similarly, would seriously doubt that all men could at any time achieve such earthly perfection.

a society in which the Rights of persons would never be violated, they would nevertheless remain coercible. Although actual use of force might never come into play, the Right to use it would still be present. How else can the validity of a Right be explained, if not by the moral and juridical possibility of enforcing it? Coercibility means just that, and nothing more.

SECTION 2. EXTENT OF COERCIBILITY

The concept of coercibility encompasses any and all means necessary to protect the Right in question. So far mention has been made only of the actual use of force to prevent the occurrence of an injury, of an injustice. Other means of coercion are available to the possessor of a Right.[77]

One of the most effective methods of warding off the violation of Right is to threaten with penalties any possible unjust invader. Common experience teaches that some men, especially in their formative years, respond more readily to the fear of punishment than to the rational attraction of good.[78] This fear, however, would lose its beneficial effects if it were not rooted in the certain knowledge that punishment is actually inflicted upon the violators of Right. A proper sense of avenging finds its rightful place in the notion of coercibility.

The vindication of a violated Right may seem, at first glance, a very ineffective measure, precisely because of its appearance *post factum.* A victim of murder, for instance, will hardly benefit from the punishment meted out to his assassin. Very unfortunately the possession of a Right is not always strengthened by the actual physical means of protecting it. Because of the social implications of Right, however, the castigation of the offender is imperative. Such a procedure not only has a remedial effect upon the troubled

[77] As will be seen in the next section, these means are most often reserved to the agencies of government in society: in that respect, they represent the possessor of the Right which they protect by law.

[78] Whatever be the views of certain modern child-psychologists, it still seems true that the fear of the rod, if tempered with parental love, is most salutary to children in their early years.

social order, but it also serves as a warning to others. It is an educational means for all those members of society not impressed by altruistic motives.

Some may offer the objection that to extol the merits of retaliation denotes a certain lack of dignity on the part of human beings. The avenging sentiment, according to them, smacks too much of the animal-like instinct in men.—A closer study of the problem reveals that not all animalistic tendencies are to be rejected. Man has much to learn from the basic instincts of animals as well as from the fundamental inclinations of nature.[79] If a dog instinctively repels anyone who attempts to take away its food, and even proceeds to inflict damage upon the aggressor, there must be a good reason for this action, a reason known to the wise Creator of the dog and its instincts. Similarly, if a man can do nothing other than simply retrieve an object stolen from his lawful possession, in what useful way does he protect his Right of ownership against future invasion? Given the possibility of imposing certain physical restrictions upon the thief, he has done something positive in the way of rendering his Right secure.

There should be, however, a distinctively human element in the exercise of physical coaction, i.e., it should be moderate and rational.[80] The Rights of an individual man are not limitless: they are restricted by the common good, by the Rights of all others in society.[81] The coercibility of Right legitimates only that amount

---

[79] "Ex rebus naturalibus ad res humanas derivatur, ut id, quod contra aliquid insurgit, ab eo detrimentum patiatur. Videmus enim in rebus naturalibus quod unum contrarium vehementius agit altero contrario superveniente. Unde et in hominibus hoc ex naturali inclinatione invenitur, ut unusquisque deprimat eum, qui contra ipsum exsurgit."—S. Thomas, *Summa Theologiae,* IaIIae, q.87, a.1.

[80] Right reason dictates that coaction may be used only when a true violation of Right has been committed. It is possible to suffer or to inflict damage without such a violation. The lawful erection of a house which obstructs a neighbor's previously broad view does not constitute a juridical violation and consequently does not admit of retribution. Cf. Bender, *Philosophia Iuris,* pp. 146-147.

[81] Since the individual is naturally prejudiced in his own favor, it would be difficult for him to temper his reaction to personal injury with the exigencies of the common good. That is one of the reasons for society to

of force which is necessary to prevent the recurrence of the violation. One must remember also that punishment, to be properly human, must aim, whenever possible, at the correction of the social offender, so that he, too, may exercise his Rights and thus achieve his own human perfection and development.[82]

SECTION 3.
EXERCISE OF COERCIBILITY

Experience and history reveal the inadequacy of the individual's means of protecting his Rights. In the first phases of juridical evolution, he enlisted the assistance of his family or clan. When the State's organization was sufficiently complete, it provided a much more suitable exercise of the coercibility of Right.[83]

The necessity of the State's intervention in this matter is drawn first from the physical incapacity of most men to protect their individual Rights. It is impossible for the ordinary man to employ guards to watch over his property and to defend his person. In the absence of society, his Right of coercibility would be most ineffective. Only the rich and the mighty could prevail upon others to respect their Rights. This would inevitably lead, in practice, to the unsound conclusion that might makes Right.

Another source of inadequacy on the part of the individual person is his usual inability to detach himself from purely subjective goods and to evaluate properly the exigencies of the objective order of justice in society. Suffering sometimes brings out the worst in men, in the sense that it arouses their passions to such a degree of turbulence as to cast a cloud over the functioning of their minds. Only the rare individual can rise above these circumstances, discern whether real injury has been inflicted and

take over the infliction of punishment, as will be explained in the next section.

[82] Olgiati has a beautiful page, inspired by Saint Thomas, on the morality of juridical coaction. He concludes: "In quanto coattività e coazione, la forza fisica, non riguardata estrinsecamente come fatto, ma valutata nel suo significato, è eticità, essendo espressione della giustizia."—*Il Concetto di Giuridicità in San Tommaso d'Aquino,* p. 200.

[83] This offers another point of proof for the sociability of man. Cf. Del Vecchio, *Philosophy of Law,* pp. 302-303.

what measures of retribution are deserved. An unbiased organization, formed by the State, stands in a much better position to judge the merits of his case. Because of the specialized learning of its members and their preparation for this task, they will perceive more clearly the real injustice done to the individual and the best way to compensate for it, with the least possible disturbance of social peace.[84] For these main reasons, the individual normally must yield the exercise of the coercibility of Right to society, to the State.

The yielding of a person's exercise of coercion does not include, however, an absolute and irrevocable loss of the Right to it. The State cannot and does not demand that the individual relinquish this Right entirely, but only restricts and regulates it in most cases for the sake of public peace and security.[85] Of the many possible ways open to the individual to protect his Rights, the State legitimately decrees that he may select, in the majority of cases, only those which are sanctioned by its own authority.

The truth stated above, i.e., regarding the individual's retention of the exercise of coercion, finds corroboration in cases of violent aggression. Even in modern society the police forces are incapable of coping with all contingencies. A citizen, for instance, retains the Right to resist physically the attack of a would-be murderer. It would be stupid of him, at that moment, to depend on society for the protection of a Right whose object is most dear to him. If he is successful in disarming the aggressor, however, his efforts at retaliation are limited to denouncing him to the public authorities for punishment. In that way, measures can be taken

[84] Cf. Bender, *op. cit.*, pp. 135-136.

[85] "Bene tamen notandum est auctoritatem publicam in rebuspublicis hodiernis, ubi exercitium iuris coactivitatis sat perfecte legibus est regulatum, non proprie *abstulisse* ius coactivitatis vel exercitium eius a personis privatis. Minime. Natura sua ius coactivitatis est in eodem subiecto, in quo est ipsum ius principale. Esset contra naturam rerum, si auctoritas socialis auferret in generali hoc ius ab omnibus membris societatis. . . . Sed propter bonum commune exercitium iuris restringitur, i.e. ex diversis modis, quibus personae privatae illud exercere possunt, unus interdicitur et alius solus permittitur, saltem pro maiori numero casuum."—Bender, *op. cit.*, p. 137.

which procure the good of society as a whole, and not only the personal satisfaction of the injured person.[86]

Considered as a moral person, the State also possesses definite Rights of its own in regard to its members and to the other States of the world. In the latter instance, the inviolability of these Rights demands at times the use of coercion by one State against another. Experience has taught man, however, the necessity of a supra-national organization competent to settle the differences between States. Much progress has been achieved in this direction in recent years, through the formation of the United Nations Organization. Humanity still yearns, however, for the day when such a union of States will possess sufficient moral and physical power to subdue the overly ambitious pretensions of those who would impose their might upon their less fortunate neighbors. By what Right or Law can and should this organization rule? The only recourse possible seems to be to natural right reason.[87]

Article IV: Laws As Norms of Right

SECTION 1.

THE GENERAL CONCEPT OF LAW[88]

The most common and popular idea of law suggests that it is a rule of action which is binding. It obliges subjects to act in a

[86] A person may also find himself in a position to vindicate certain Rights against the State considered as a moral person. Where the positive law of that State permits and regulates such an action, no difficulty arises. What recourse, however, does a person have when the State does not admit such an action against itself? (Such circumstances are not unheard of in modern States). The common good will most often require that the injured person suffer in silence. Only in extraordinary circumstances (to be outlined *below*, pp. 154-162) should one contemplate open rebellion and resistance to the State.

[87] Again the present writer insinuates what will be treated in the following article and throughout the dissertation, namely that the Natural Law is the fundamental norm of Right. In this case it does not exclude, but it rather demands, the elaboration of a positive law among the various States, which is called International Law. Cf. Del Vecchio, *Philosophy of Law*, pp. 303-304; Bender, *Philosophia Iuris*, pp. 141-142.

[88] The writer prefers to give here only the general notion of law. A

certain manner, or to refrain from doing so. In this very generic sense, laws may be said to apply to inanimate as well as animate beings, to animals as well as men. The predominant element in all these laws is that of necessity. The physicists refer to the laws of nature, such as that of gravity, as being necessary. In the same manner, animals are said to be *driven* by their instincts, which are but the expression of their nature.

On a higher level, the laws affecting man's conscious behavior take on a different aspect of necessity. Every human being realizes that his subjection to laws, v.g., to the laws of a State, differs considerably from that of two bodies to the law of gravity. Whereas the laws of nature impose a physical necessity upon the beings they affect, laws for men do not.[89] The distinctive quality of human laws, in other words, lies in their intellectual content. They are, as it were, an appeal to man's intelligence and free will. One should not conclude, however, that human laws have no cogent force, but only that the latter takes on a different character. Instead of being physical it is moral, i.e., conditioned by man's relation to the purpose of these laws. Such laws, consequently, are called moral laws, at least in a wide sense.

Everybody recognizes the existence of laws which impose only a conditional necessity. The laws of architecture, v.g., bind only those who want to build something, and build it well. Only true artists, similarly, will submit to the rules of art. One cannot say indiscriminately that such rules apply to all men; they apply to only those who wish to achieve the specific purpose of these rules.[90]

One law, however, to which all men must adhere is the law of rationality, the law of their very being.[91] Man must live as a man, i.e., as one who is aware of his noble destiny as a rational

---

more detailed study will appear in the following chapters on the Natural and Positive laws.

[89] Physical coercion may serve to enforce a law, but the law itself has no physically coercive power of its own.

[90] Such laws are called "moral" laws in the wide sense, in opposition to those which necessarily bind all men. Only the latter will receive full discussion in the following pages.

[91] As will be shown in the next chapter, this is, in substance, the Natural Law, a manifestation of the eternal law of God.

being. He cannot escape this responsibility without denying himself, without denying his nature. He has no choice in this matter: his refusal to act rationally would amount to a renunciation of his freedom, of that intellectual faculty which distinguishes him from animals and other non-rational beings.[92]

The rational nature of man entails many consequences of moral import. The first of these consists in man's humble recognition of his subjection to God and to God's laws.[93] Man understands that he is rational only because he was made so by God who is Reason personified. He realizes that he is not abdicating his autonomy, but really asserting it, by ascribing its origin to God.[94] He perceives, furthermore, that his greatness and nobility depend essentially upon a practical recognition of God's sovereignty over him and all things of the world. The homage and respect which he pays to God do not detract in any way from his human dignity, no more than the homage and respect of a son for his father.[95]

In the final analysis, man admits that his true dignity lies in his resemblance, however remote, to God, and, therefore, that his true perfection will consist in following as closely as possible the laws of God. With confidence in the intellectual powers received from God, he will endeavor to study his own nature and

[92] Man's free will is based on reason. Where the latter falls prey to inordinate passions, the whole personality of man is somewhat enslaved by matter, submerged into things that are beneath his dignity. Only when his mind dominates matter does man properly exercise his free will, accepting deliberately the responsibilities of life and choosing freely the best means to attain perfection.

[93] For a complete philosophical explanation, see the masterful work of Garrigou-Lagrange, *God, His Existence and His Nature; a Thomistic Solution of Certain Agnostic Antinomies,* trans. from 5. ed. by Dom Bede Rose (St. Louis: B. Herder, 1934, 1936). Another very penetrating study, less scholastic in technique, is that of Henri de Lubac, *Sur les chemins de Dieu* (Aubier: Editions Montaigne, 1956).

[94] The learned scientist loses no self-respect by referring with pride to a world-renowned teacher as a source of his knowledge in a particular field. So also should men be proud of their dependence upon God in the realm of being and rationality.

[95] Although outside the scope of philosophy, it is significant that Divine Revelation teaches that all men are brothers who have the same God for a Father. Cf., v.g., Mt. VI, 25-34; Rom., VIII, 14-17; I Jn., III.

thus discern the designs of God for him and for his happiness.[96] In a similar manner, since he is associated with God in the government of the world, he will analyze the intimate nature of other creatures and strive to utilize them in the best way possible, always respecting the order which he finds there. In brief, man's reason, a divine gift, imposes upon him the duty of submission and devotion to God, of respect and love for Him.

The rationality of man must also assert itself in the realm of self-government.[97] Inasmuch as man is a composite being, his activity necessarily reflects something of both the body and the soul.[98] Although the senses and passions play an important role they must be controlled by reason. This is precisely the essence of virtue, and only a virtuous man is fully a man. The laws of man's natural dignity requiring the exercise of the virtues of temperance, fortitude and prudence (and their integral components) are observed only when reason has the upper hand in the conduct of a person's life. The laws of individual behavior, to which all men must conform, depend therefore upon the law of reason in man.

There are other laws to which man must submit as a result of his rational nature: the law of sociality and consequently the laws of society. The law of sociality, perceived by human reason, is but the expression of man's need for the society of his fellowmen. This law gives rise to many other rules of conduct according to which men must live if their association is to prove helpful.[99]

---

[96] The rational being who is in close relation with God and who obeys His laws will conceive a profound desire to know Him and to love Him more fully. Beyond this goal of natural attraction, Revelation discloses that man, through divine kinship in grace, is called to an even greater fulfillment consisting in the vision and fruition of God in His essence. Cf., v.g., Mt. V, 3-12; Luke, VI, 20-23; I Cor., XIII, 11-13.

[97] Man is studied here in an absolute manner, i.e., in himself alone, without consideration of other intellectual beings with whom he lives.

[98] Even man's most spiritual thoughts are dependent upon the senses and cannot be expressed except in sensible symbols.

[99] It should be noted that, even before the establishment of concrete societies or States, there already existed laws formulated by reason for the inter-activity of mankind as a whole. This observation leads to the

Circumstances of a historical nature determine the grouping of men according to certain territorial boundaries, thus forming separate societies with their own systems of law and order. Right reason dictates that men must adhere to these in order to secure their full development and happiness.[100]

The laws affecting human behavior can therefore be classified into three groups: the laws governing man's relationship to God, to himself and to his fellowmen in society. It is to all three sets of laws that the rationality of man requires that he submit himself. To which law is Right related and in what manner: this is the object of the next section.

SECTION 2.
RELATION OF RIGHT TO LAWS

From the preceding articles of this chapter, it is clear that only those laws which govern man's social life have a bearing on Right. Only in an improper manner can one speak of Rights between God and man, because of the infinite inequality between them.[101] Because of their normative character, reasonable social laws, whether natural or positive, are the efficient cause of the Rights of men. They rule over the activity of men in such a way as to decree what is the extent of Right between them; they establish the objective order of justice which must reign among them.[102] As a result, certain Rights are attributed to some people, to which correspond obligations of respect on the part of others. Only those laws are, therefore, properly called juridical, which govern the Rights of men in society.[103]

From this viewpoint, one notices the difference between the

---

conclusion that not all laws of social life have their origin in the State. See *below*, section 3, pp. 37ff.

100 Reason demands society in general, not any society in particular. States and empires come and go, but the law of sociality remains.

101 There is certainly no reciprocity of Rights between these two. One may, however, speak of the Rights of God when implying man's duty of subjection to God's laws. See *above*, p. 20, n. 52.

102 It is presupposed that they are the product of reason in conformity with the common good of man, i.e., in conformity with the Natural Law.

103 From its Latin roots, juridical means to establish Right: *ius dicere.*

divine and human legislators. God's view is all-embracing, envisioning man's complete good and perfection. Through the light of reason instilled in men, He is able to direct the whole of man's activity. His laws govern not only the order of justice which must reign in society, but also the perfection of the individual considered in an absolute manner, without reference to society. Thus He commands the observance of the laws of temperance, fortitude and prudence. His legislation similarly deals with man's relations with God Himself.

The field of vision open to the human legislator is much more narrow. His sole objective is the securing of the common good of the society which he governs, the maintaining of social justice. His power over individuals is limited to their perfection as citizens of the particular society over which he rules. Whatever he commands must have some necessary link with the good of his subjects as a whole. Human legislators do enact laws which at first glance seem to concern only the individual as such. They regulate, for instance, the sale of liquor, especially to minors. This should not be considered as an illegitimate invasion of private conscience, because these measures ultimately have the common good in view.[104]

One must not, for that matter, labor under the false impression that the human legislator has concern only for the external actions of men. He cannot and does not consider his subjects as mechanical robots. To be sure, because of his human limitations, his view is directed to the external manifestation of the will of men. He must be convinced, however, that the common good, his primary objective, will not live up to its name if it does not develop virtue and perfection in the persons of his community.[105] Some obvious examples of the human lawmaker's consideration for internal actions are found in the regulations affecting contracts, where the intention of the parties plays a vital role. The same observation is possible in the field of penal law, where punishment is meted

[104] Cf. Bender, *Philosophia Iuris*, p. 119-121.

[105] No social order can possibly subsist without the virtuous dispositions of the citizens. Education should strive to replace fear with virtue as a motive for the observance of laws.

out in proportion to the intent and responsibility of the culprit. insofar as this is possible.[106]

SECTION 3.
POSITIVE LAW IS NOT THE SOLE CAUSE OF RIGHT

Throughout this first chapter, the idea of Right has been assimilated to that of justice, i.e., the obligation of rendering to others what is due to them. The purpose of this special section is to emphasize that Right and justice are not the creation of the State, that there exist Rights other than those conferred upon individuals by particular societies.

The basis of this affirmation lies in the fact that men are not the creatures of the State, but that the State is the creature of men. Over and above his subjection to one State in particular, man is affiliated with the universal society of mankind. Reason imposes upon him, as a man, certain duties and obligations toward his fellowmen which are independent of the State to which he belongs. Long before States existed in their modern form of legislative government, man knew that to avoid homicide and dishonesty was a necessary condition for his association with others. He respected, consequently, the Rights of others in this respect. The Right of association itself, of grouping into particular societies, is evidently antecedent to the State, since it is the justifying foundation of its very existence. Can we say, then, that because the modern State has taken over, for the most part, the protection of these Rights, it is the initial cause of them? Surely not.[107]

The logical conclusion from the foregoing is the admission of the dependence of the State upon the fundamental juridical principles of right reason. If the modern State may be legitimately called the source of Rights, it is only by reason of its respect for the basic Rights of man already demanded by his own rational

[106] See the interesting remarks of Del Vecchio, *Philosophy of Law*, pp. 255-260.

[107] For practical purposes, international law is still at a rudimentary stage, at the stage of private justice, pending the formation of a superstatal State. And yet, one cannot say that there is no international justice. Why should there be any clamor of injustice, then, when one of the parties to a treaty fails to live up to its promises?

nature and the nature of things. In other words, positive law is an outgrowth of the Natural Law.[108] Some of the Rights and duties imposed on man by the Natural Law pertain therefore to the juridical order no less certainly than do the Rights and duties established by the positive laws.

It is therefore incorrect to advocate a complete divorce of the juridical order from the moral order. The latter is all-inclusive, regulating the entire sphere of man's activity in regard to necessary ends, and seeking the full development of man's potentialities. Under its objective of the ultimate good of man, it embraces all the particular goods which lead to it. One of these is the good of social justice so necessary to man, which good is assured by the juridical order. No clear-cut separation can be effected between the two orders, because the juridical order forms an integral part of the moral order. There exists, however, a valid distinction between the two: not every moral obligation is juridical, i.e., concerned with the relations of one man to others in society.

The opinion which advocates a complete separation between the two orders is not unlike that which would declare the total incompetency of morals in economic, political and artistic matters. To be sure, the latter involve certain techniques which, considered only as such, would prove independent of moral considerations. But since they are techniques affecting the lives and destinies of human beings, they must concur, at least to that extent, with the laws of morality. In a similar manner, the juridical order comprises a whole system of enactments dealing with matters of expediency and utility which, as such, do not come directly under the moral law. The law in the United States requiring motorists to drive habitually on the right side of the road rather than on the left is a clear example of this. The manner of this determination matters not at all to morals, but the necessity of some determination can be traced back (through a long process of reasoning) to the moral law of safeguarding one's own life and that of others. Inasmuch as the moral order controls the ends to which the prac-

[108] This is true historically as well as philosophically.—This point introduces the study of these two laws, which will take place in the two following chapters of this dissertation.

tical determinations of the juridical order are meant to lead, to separate the latter from the former would be equivalent to separating the body from the head.[109]

[109] "Nous ne sommes pas sans savoir que d'aucuns entendent les (morale et droit) séparer tout-à-fait, comme on a voulu séparer la morale de l'économie, la morale de la politique ou de l'art. Dans tous ces cas, il s'agirait de techniques indépendantes, auxquelles la morale n'aurait pas à dicter des lois. Mais à y réfléchir, on devrait se rendre compte qu'une telle conception est éminemment irrationnelle et inhumaine. Il s'agit là de techniques, assurément, mais de techniques de la vie. Or la vie ne va point au hasard; elle tend vers des fins qui constituent, réunies, la destinée heureuse, et c'est à la moralité générale, aux moeurs, qu'il appartient de réaliser ces fins. Toutes les techniques qui confèrent au bonheur ou au malheur des hommes rentrent donc sous la loi de la moralité, ont des comptes à lui rendre, ce qui ne signifie pas qu'elles se confondent avec elle. La morale, si l'on y fait abstraction de la justice, qu'il s'agit de lui comparer, définit le devoir par rapport aux dispositions de l'individu qui agit. Par exemple, je suis tempérant si je mange d'après mon appétit. Je suis prudent en matière de sport si je m'exerce en tenant compte de mes forces et ainsi du reste. Le droit, lui, est objectif: il est relatif à un état de fait; quelles que soient les dispositions du sujet, il vaut par lui-même. Et, en outre, il est appelé à édicter des lois d'utilité au sujet desquelles la morale n'aurait ni compétence ni autorité propre. La morale s'occupe de ce qui est honnête, le droit de ce qui est à la fois utile et juste; or l'honnête, et le juste, l'honnête et l'utile surtout ne se recouvrent pas. Au surplus, le droit ne s'inquiète directement que des actions extérieures qui seules viennent en société, de l'intérieur uniquement pour qualifier et quasi identifier l'acte extérieur. Si l'acte intérieur devait rester en lui-même, on ne s'en occuperait pas. La morale, au contraire, s'occupe surtout du dedans et du dehors uniquement comme achèvement de réalisation et comme témoignage. Il y a donc distinction très nette. Mais toujours est-il qu'on ne peut séparer ces deux disciplines. La morale domine le droit, contrôle ses déterminations, dirige sa marche et juge des fins qu'il poursuit. . . ." —Sertillanges, *La philosophie des lois*, Collections d'Essais "Faits et Idées," Vol. II (Paris: Editions Alsatia, 1946), pp. 40-41.—On this important point, see also Van Overbeke, "De Relatione Ordinem Iuridicum inter et Ordinem Moralem," *Ephemerides Theologicae Lovanienses*, XI (1934), pp. 289-346; Bender, *Philosophia Iuris*, pp. 223-238; Del Vecchio, *Philosophy of Law*, pp. 263-276.

CHAPTER II: THE NATURAL LAW

This second chapter purports to establish the existence, and to throw some light on the essence and content of the Natural Law.[1] Here and there in the first chapter, especially in the last article, reference has been made to the notion of a Law distinct from the written codes of Law now in force in various States.[2] The reader may have scored such a reference as unwarranted, inasmuch as it took for granted the existence of such a Law. Besides the cursory justification given in the text, the assumption was not entirely gratuitous. Alexander Passerin d'Entrèves states:

> "For over two thousand years the idea of natural law has played a prominent part in thought and in history. It was conceived as the ultimate measure of right and wrong, as the pattern of the good life or 'life according to nature.' It provided a potent incentive to reflection, the touchstone of existing institutions, the justification of conservatism as well as of revolution." [3]

---

[1] The writer is well aware that hundreds of more enlightened students have preceded him in this field. Even if his discussion has little originality to its credit, he hopes that, in view of the extreme importance and timeliness of the subject itself, his efforts at elucidating the concept of the Natural Law will not prove entirely useless.

[2] It should be noted immediately that "Natural Law" has in English two connotations. It is used first in the sense of the body of natural and moral laws governing man's entire rational activity, i.e., in respect to God, to himself and to his fellowmen (*lex naturalis, loi naturelle, legge naturale*). A second meaning attaches to "Natural Law" when it denotes exclusively the regulation of man's actions in the legal and social sphere (*ius naturale, droit naturel, diritto naturale*). Unless the contrary is clearly indicated in the text or the context, it is exclusively the second meaning that is intended here. Cf. Messner, *Social Ethics*, p. 15; *supra*, p. 7, n. 15.

[3] *Natural Law, An Introduction to Legal Philosophy* (London: Hutchinson's University Library, 1951), p. 6. The writer professes much admiration for this author's penetrating insight into the humanizing function of the Natural Law idea through the centuries.

Despite the acute criticisms lodged against it by a number of past and contemporary authors, the notion of a Natural Law lives on, and has gained many new recruits among the philosophers of Law.[4]

Article I: Existence of the Natural Law

SECTION 1. NECESSITY OF THE NATURAL LAW[5]

It has been shown that laws are the norms of Right, i.e., all Rights find their basis in laws or in some system of laws. Even the so-called "Rights of man," v.g., freedom of conscience, of religion, the Rights to one's own life, to one's honor, all these must have their foundation in Law. It is not enough for man to assert his freedoms: he must justify them in some way. A liquor dealer for example, must be able to exhibit a license obtained from the State in order to vindicate his Right to exercise this trade. Whenever the legitimacy of his practice is questioned, he immediately refers to the law which establishes and supports it. The reaction of the ordinary person is not quite the same whenever there is a dispute over his Right to live, for instance. Never will he admit that it is only because the State has so decreed that others must respect his life, his body or his person.[6] In some manner,

[4] See, v.g., Messner, *op. cit.*, pp. 235-245, where he discusses "The Modern Movement Towards Natural Law" (§ 54).

[5] In the previous chapter, the writer has already alluded to some of the arguments proposed in the following pages.

[6] The Supreme Court of the United States had much the same opinion in a particular case: "It must be conceded that there are . . . rights in every free government beyond the control of the State. A government which *recognized* no such rights, which held the lives, the liberty, and the property of its citizens subject at all times to the absolute disposition and unlimited control of even the most democratic depository of power, is after all but a despotism. It is true it is a despotism of the many, of the majority, if you choose to call it so, but it is none the less a despotism."—*Citizens' Savings & Loan Association v. Topeka*, 20 Wall. 665, 662, 22L, Ed. 455 (1874); cited by Corwin, "Natural Law and Constitutional Law," in *University of Notre Dame Natural Law Institute Proceedings* (Indiana: College of Law, University of Notre Dame), III (1949), 62. Italics are the writer's.

whether clear or obscure, he will appeal to another Law, based more directly upon the dignity of the human being. His appeal to such a Law will be in accord with the battle that millions of men have fought through the centuries for the recognition of what they considered to be their proper human Rights. Men of all ages have been convinced that their rulers had no power over these Rights, except to protect them and regulate them for the common good of the community.

One of the objectives of civic education is to teach men docile submission to the laws of the particular society in which they live. Even the most modest sense of inquisitiveness will lead them to inquire regarding the why and wherefore of this attitude of docility. All men being equal by nature, there must be some ulterior foundation for the authority of one man or a group of men over others. In virtue of what power can the individual subject be required to adhere to laws enacted by other men? Should he not be allowed to make his own decisions, to rule his own life, in the manner which he deems fit? To answer this question by saying that as a matter of fact there are positive laws enforced by the police is to answer it not at all. The recourse to physical force does not satisfy the human mind, which contends that men are unlike sheep led by the staff of the shepherd.

The only alternative open to the educator is a direct appeal to a higher and superior source of authority, to a Law which transcends the individual as such. Since no solution can be reached at the level of individual men (all men being equal), recourse must be had to the common nature of men and the course of action it indicates.[7] Since men cannot rationally deny their nature, they must be ruled by it. By virtue of this nature they are obliged to unite as members in a society. The fundamental laws of society, and especially the obligations deriving through its own particular positive laws, trace their roots, consequently, to the Law of human nature: what men for centuries have called the Natural Law.

For some strange reason unintelligible to the present writer, there are some authors who, while they are willing to admit the

[7] Ultimately, the source of authority is God, the Creator of human nature, as will be explained further in the second article of this chapter.

existence of the Natural Law, refuse to give it the juridical impact it demands. They refer to it as the Natural *moral* Law, in opposition to positive laws called strictly juridical. The logical consequences of this doctrine seem quite ridiculous. The very obligation of subjects to obey laws and the authority of the human legislator to impose them would be merely moral. That is to say that the latter could simply exhort citizens to adhere to his rules, without having the Right (strictly juridical) to enforce them physically.[8]

The denial of the Natural Law leads to the necessity of recognizing the absolute validity or justice of all laws enacted by human governments.[9] One cannot measure the perfection of a being without comparing it with some superior model of perfection. Nor can one qualify a law as being just or unjust except by reference to some higher norm of conduct or legislation. If in a certain locality the governor has decreed, for example, that when the sun passes over this locality it will be midday, then the sun can never be early or tardy: it cannot pass except on the stroke of twelve noon.[10] If the positive law is supreme in the field of Law, it cannot fail to be just. There is hardly a historian who would subscribe to such a conclusion.

The argument proposed above should not be construed as an indictment against legislators. One can believe in the good judgment and good will of rulers without setting them up as gods. It is to be hoped and expected that they have the best interests of society at heart. No one cares to challenge their desire to establish laws which will make for the best possible order of harmony and peace. But they will be forced to admit that no order can be achieved among various and multiple elements without recourse

[8] Cf. Bender, *Philosophia Iuris*, pp. 165-166. How also could the so-called "Rights of Man," which are founded on the Natural Law, be true Rights, i.e., susceptible to violation on the part of others. It seems that the view now being criticized stems from the separation of Right from morals along with the confusion resulting from such an unsound position. On the latter point, cf. *supra*, pp. 38-39.

[9] This abstract statement takes on an odious character if applied to concrete cases of legislative aberration. One would be forced to justify, for instance, the massacre of the Holy Innocents by Herod.

[10] Appropriate example given by Bender, *op. cit.*, p. 167.

to a principle of unity. It would be futile to search elsewhere than in the very nature of men and society for this principle of unity, i.e., in the Natural Law.[11]

Another argument favoring the necessity of a Natural Law flows from the radical insufficiency of positive law itself.[12] The latter is, in fact, a law laid down for the majority of cases, ordinary cases. The legislator simply cannot foresee in a general law all the possible circumstances which could render his law inapplicable in a given situation. Another principle of effectiveness requires that positive laws possess a character of stability and permanency. There inevitably ensues an opposition between fixed statutes and the changing pattern of social life. The wisdom of a lawmaker should induce him to relinquish a certain power of *adjustment* to the officers in charge of applying the law. To be sure, the main ambition of the jurist should be to interpret the law in such a way that it still retains some of its force. Whenever this becomes impossible in serving the cause of justice, he will make use of the fundamental principles of Right outlined in the

---

[11] Cf. Renard, *Le Droit, la Justice et la Volonté* (Paris: Recueil Sirey, 1924), pp. 88-91. "A l'arrière des lois et des coutumes, de la jurisprudence et de la doctrine, par-dessous les constructions de la dialectique juridique, au delà des intérêts légitimes à la garde desquels veillent la police et les tribunaux, soutenant les uns et les autres comme le roc enfoui dans la terre soutient le monument qui se dresse au soleil,—il y a un Droit éternel et immuable, enraciné dans la nature spécifique de l'homme, révélé par sa droite raison, reflet elle-même de la Raison divine. Droit immuable, soubassement unique et universel de tous les droits historiques, de tous les droits nationaux, de tous les droits spéciaux: je sais bien que c'est la "vieille chanson"; je lui ai même, tant elle est vieille, délivré un brevet d'éternité. Je sais bien que la mode l'a balayée, la "vieille chanson." Seulement, il se produit dans l'histoire de l'humanité des coups de tonnerre qui balayent la mode; leur fracas étouffe les nouvelles chansons, et les sceptiques rentrent dans leur trou. A ce moment, la vieille chanson rebondit; elle éclate d'un bout à l'autre du pays; à ses accents, une génération reconnaît en elle-même ce qu'il y a de plus fièrement humain, et s'offre en holocauste pour la victoire du Droit." Idem, *Le Droit, l'Ordre et la Raison* (Paris: Recueil Sirey, 1927), pp. 18-19.

[12] The writer considers it useful to the purpose at hand to anticipate somewhat on this point what belongs properly to the third chapter.

Natural Law.[13] One of the characteristics of the Natural Law is its resiliency: whenever there occurs a breakage or a *lacuna* in the positive law, the Natural Law bounces back to the surface and suggests the appropriate rule of conduct.[14]

One of the principal objections lodged against the juridicity of the Natural Law lies in the assertion that it is devoid of coercibility. The weakness of this argument goes back to an incorrect definition of coercibility. The latter is not defined as the physical power, but as the *moral* power or legitimacy of using physical coercion.[15] No one will deny that long before the existence of well regulated Societies man was lawfully entitled to defend the basic Rights which he possessed as a man.[16] At the root of the objection now being studied there rests a misconception of the role of Natural Law in society. The Natural Law is not and cannot be a system which stands by itself and is completely separated from that of positive law.[17] Nowhere does it exist except in concrete society,

---

[13] "Il y a et il ne peut pas ne pas y avoir des créations doctrinales ou jurisprudentielles 'de toutes pièces.' Ici la doctrine et la jurisprudence passent au premier rang des sources du droit. Il leur appartient d'interroger les réalités sociales, les besoins et les intérêts, de les confronter avec l'idéal de Justice et de droit naturel auquel je ne me lasse de revenir, de s'inspirer de ce bon sens pratique que développent l'expérience des affaires et la méditation philosophique, et puis de se risquer à faire du nouveau."—Renard, *Le Droit, La Justice et la Volonté*, pp. 43-44.

[14] Renard gives the example of an institution (moral person) from which the State should, for one reason or another, retract its juridical sanction. What would happen to the property owned by this corporation? Can it be confiscated by the State? Evidently not, but on no other basis save common sense dictated by the Natural Law.—*Op. cit.*, pp. 155-160.

[15] Cf. *supra*, pp. 25-27.

[16] Bender, to whose observations the writer reverts here, offers the clear example of Abel being attacked by Cain. No police protection was available at that time, but men of all ages will look upon Cain's assault as a true injury (in the juridical sense of the word). No one, furthermore, will dispute Abel's Right to protect himself, a Right he would have undoubtedly exercised, had he found himself in more favorable circumstances.—*Op. cit.* pp. 173-175.

[17] ". . . one must be on guard against the idea as though Natural Law were a code of hard and fast rules, existing, as it were, on the second story of the building above the first floor of positive law."—Kuttner,

the existence of which constitutes its first postulate. And precisely one of the exigencies behind this postulate is the necessity of regulating the use of coercion.[18]

SECTION 2.
WHY SOME MODERN JURISTS REJECT THE NATURAL LAW

In view of the sound arguments supporting the existence of a supra-positive law, it is difficult to grasp the refusal of so many modern jurists to accept the idea of a Natural Law. For some it is perhaps because they are so engrossed in the field of positive law that they have little time or inclination to study its sources. As Lawson puts it:

> "There is a common tendency on the part of jurists—it has been very strong at many periods in the past—to feel that a legal system can be rationally satisfying by its mere elegance and the internal logic governing the relations between its parts. From this point of view, a legal system is a sort of logical machine; and a machine may be judged by the simplicity and smoothness of its running. I think everyone will sympathize with this point of view; but there is danger of becoming fascinated by the beauty of a machine which one makes constantly more perfect for a specialized purpose. The machine tends to exist in and for itself and to acquire a greater importance than the purpose it was meant to fulfill; and the purpose itself often disappears."[19]

It would seem, in brief, that all jurists should intend to serve the cause of justice itself rather than devote their exclusive attention to the means originally designed to achieve that purpose.[20]

"Natural Law and Canon Law," *University of Notre Dame Natural Law Institute Proceedings* (Indiana: College of Law, University of Notre Dame), III (1949), 100.

[18] Cf. *supra*, pp. 29-31.

[19] *The Rational Strength of English Law* (London: Stevens & Sons, Ltd., 1951), p. 13.

[20] For a good picture of the revival of Natural Law especially in America, see Pacifico Ortiz & Arthur A. North, "A Return to the Natural Law," *Thought*, XXX (Winter, 1955-1956), n. 119, pp. 525-536.

Perhaps many of the modern scholars reject the Natural Law because they feel the need to react violently against the doctrine expounded by philosophers of the 17th and 18th centuries. It is not surprising that intelligent men refuse to adhere to a Natural Law code comprising rationalistically deduced prescriptions which regulate "all legal spheres down to the minutest detail." [21] The positivistic legal mind could not help but discard, similarly, the sentimental theory according to which all the principles of the Natural Law are engraved in the hearts of men, and therefore completely self-evident to all.[22] The doctrine of Natural Law most severely attacked by these authors is not the traditional doctrine founded on facts, on the true nature of men, but one which is rooted in an imaginary state of nature existing before man's participation in society.[23] Although the practice may be thought quite

---

[21] Rommen, *The Natural Law, A Study in Legal and Social History and Philosophy* (trans. by Thomas R. Hanley, St. Louis & London: B. Herder Book Co., 1947), p. 217. According to the author, "scarcely more than the formal decree of the legislator would be needed to transform them into codes of positive law."—*Loc. cit.*

[22] H. A. Taine (1828-1843), who in 1857 published *Les Philosophes classiques du XIXe siécle en France*, criticized this theory thus: "Je ne vois pas votre droit naturel, écrit-il. Vous dites qu'il est gravé dans tous les coeurs; je ne vois rien de gravé dans mon coeur. Vous dites qu'il est évident et palpable, parce qu'il consiste en faits d'une démonstration facile pour chacun; mais je ne vois pas que vous démontriez rien du tout. Vous dites qu'il est universel et que nous ne pouvons nous empêcher de le reconnaître; comment alors le droit varie-t-il de peuple à peuple? En réalité tout ce que vous dites est arbitraire. C'est une doctrine de bourgeois satisfait qui tâche de sauvegarder l'ordre dont il profite, en le couvrant de l'ombre d'une divinité dont nous ne savons si elle existe."—Quoted by Leclercq, *Leçons de droit naturel*, I, 34.

[23] Thirty years ago L. Le Fur (1870-1943) wrote: "Aujourd'hui encore, beaucoup de ceux qui critiquent le droit naturel . . . s'en prennent spécialement aux théories philosophiques du XVIIIe siècle, à celle de Rousseau notamment, avec ses invraisemblances d'un état de nature antérieur à la vie en société et d'un droit naturel immuable; après quoi ils condamnent en bloc toutes les théories sur le droit naturel, sans paraître se rendre compte que leurs arguments ne visent qu'une déviation manifeste de la théorie traditionnelle, et qu'ils englobent dans une même et sommaire réprobation des théories qui parfois . . . sont précisément opposées."—"La théorie du droit naturel depuis le XVIIe siècle et la doctrine moderne," *Recueil des*

fashionable in certain circles, the condemning of all theories of Natural Law for the reason that some misguided philosophers have used its name in vain with a view to covering up fantastic hypotheses is poor logic indeed. That the idea of Natural Law is a perfectly valid one is supported by the unquestionable influence it has exercised in the shaping of positive institutes of law. One author admirably states:

> "It would never have occurred to a political theorist in the Middle Ages to doubt that the whole aim of law was approximation to ideal justice, or to regard particular laws merely as rules of thumb for the mechanical regulation of society. It was because they found in human law an aspiration towards ideal justice that the men of the Middle Ages were so deeply concerned with the Law of Nature. It has become the fashion to treat their speculation as chimerical fantasy; that it was much more than that is sufficiently shown by the influence of the Law of Nature on subsequent theory and practice. If medieval doctrines in this kind were vague and mystical, yet they contemplated an ideal with which the world cannot yet dispense. Our methods today are more empirical and less abstract; but if modern lawyers rightly distrust generalizations about natural justice and 'justice as between man and man,' that is only because in the process of time most of our rules of law have shaped themselves as justice and utility demand, and it is not usually necessary to travel beyond settled doctrine into unsettled hypothesis." [24]

Seeking the fundamental reason behind the denial of the Natural Law, one finds it in the rejection of metaphysics. The latter is the science of being and reality; not of beings in their concrete individuality and accidental forms or circumstances of existence, but in their constant and universal reality which can be abstracted

Cours de l'Académie de Droit International, p. 333; quoted by Leclercq, *Leçons de droit naturel,* I, 35.

[24] Allen, *Law in the Making* (Oxford: Clarendon Press, 1927), p. 195. See also O'Sullivan, "The Natural Law and the Common Law," *The University of Notre Dame Natural Law Institute Proceedings* (Indiana: College of Law, Notre Dame University), III (1949), 9-44.

and studied by the intellect. No one, surprisingly enough, rejects mathematics; and yet it too depends upon the method of abstraction.

> "The object of mathematical knowledge is . . . being whether real or conceptual, under the aspect of quantity itself or of quantitative relations of order and measure. Its specific light —abstraction and definition with intelligible matter alone— is a type of visualization in which not only are the conditions of singularity removed, but every reference to the perceptions of the outer senses, yet in which the object is seen and defined by the intellect only in reference, direct or indirect, to the possibility of a sensible construction by the intuitive imagination." [25]

Positivism, in theory, does not recognize as scientific any knowledge beyond that which can be acquired through the senses. It can never, therefore, assert what men should do; but only what they actually do. Sociologists of that school have much to tell about the behavior of men in society, but they can never decide what is best for them or for society.[26] Philosophers who follow this trend of thought must be satisfied with a study of comparative law, very valuable indeed, but hardly the basis of law and morality.[27]

It is impossible, in this modest work, to give a full justification of the scientific method of metaphysics.[28] One could point out, however, that the process of abstraction and the practice of gen-

[25] Maritain, *A Preface to Metaphysics, Seven Lectures on Being* (New York: Sheed & Ward, 1948), pp. 82-83.

[26] Positivistic sociologists have not always abided by this rule of their science. The illogical moralism of Durkheim (1858-1917), for instance, has been soundly criticized by Deploige in his *Le Conflit de la morale et de la sociologie* (3. ed., Paris: Nouvelle Librairie Nationale, 1923).

[27] ". . . le droit comparé, à la nouvelle mode, a la prétention de remplacer le droit naturel; et c'est là une prétention bien conservatrice, puisqu'elle encercle l'idéal du droit positif dans ses réalisations actuellement acquises: adapté aux sciences morales, le positivisme, sous toutes ses formes, est condamné à demeurer une doctrine de stagnation."—Renard, *Le Droit, l'Ordre et la Raison*, p. 108.

[28] One could consult, v.g., Maritain, *Les Degrés du Savoir*, pp. 137-484.

eralization (which form, in substance, the metaphysical method) are in everyday use among men of all walks of life. When the ordinary man speaks of "man" and "animal," and makes such statements as "man is not simply an animal," he gives conclusive evidence that he is capable of abstracting the nature of man and that of animal from the concrete beings that exist. Nowhere do "man" and "animal" exist as such, and yet they appear to common sense as being very valid concepts of reality. With the possibility of studying man as man and society as society, there follows a better understanding of the constant and natural tendencies of man, the very exigencies of his nature and that of society. From this knowledge derives the Natural Law, i.e., the body of primary principles governing the obligatory conduct of men towards one another.[29]

Article II: The Essence of the Natural Law

Throughout the last twenty pages, the writer has referred repeatedly to a norm or set of norms called upon to serve as the primary measure and foundation of all laws and all Rights. In this connection, mention has been frequently made either of the law of rationality, or of right reason, or of a supra-statal law, or of the Natural Law. In every instance the intention was to manifest the existence of an absolute criterion of justice in Law.[30] When

[29] "La doctrine classique (du droit naturel) se fait, au contraire, de la comparaison des jurisprudences, comme de toute autre expérimentation, un simple instrument de recherche pour pénétrer toujours plus avant dans la nature de l'homme, ses exigences et ses aptitudes,—un système d'indices à interpréter dans le sens d'un perfectionnement ininterrompu vers un idéal de parfaite adaptation à la nature humaine définitivement déchiffrée et adéquatement satisfaite."—Renard, *op. cit.*, p. 108.

[30] The term *absolute* should not frighten anyone. The science of Law, like all sciences, requires a stable and unchangeable criterion if it is to engender any form of certitude. "If, for instance, the original measure of length . . . were capable of becoming longer or shorter, or at least of changing without our knowing it, or being able to allow for such change, then measurement would become absolutely impossible."—M. Cronin, *The Science of Ethics* (4. ed., 2 vols., Dublin: M. H. Gill and Son, Ltd., 1939), I, 127-128.

and how does reason take on the quality of being *right* reason? What does the term Natural Law really mean? The present article proposes to answer these and other related questions.

SECTION 1.
NATURE AND THE NATURAL LAW

Even before the progress of the experimental sciences, especially sociology and ethnology, it was demonstrated that men differ considerably in their mode of living, according to race, time and locality. In some instances the variations appear so striking that they have led some to believe that a truly scientific study of man must deal with him exclusively on the individual level. More perspicacious observers contend, however, that despite the wide range of particularities mentioned above, men of all ages and places present certain clear-cut characteristics which set them off in a category of beings all their own.[31]

Not only the findings of modern science but also the simple data of common experience reveal the special nature of man, the composition of animality and rationality inherent in him. Wherever he may be, man distinguishes himself by his reflective endeavor to transform the conditions of his material existence and to explain the phenomena of physical nature.[32] His reasoning powers enable him to discover the finality of things, to grasp the proper direction certain beings must take, especially human beings, in order to achieve their fullest development. Such an investiga-

[31] "Uniforme et pleine de répétitions! telle est en somme l'histoire universelle dans ses grandes lignes, car l'âme humaine présente partout une grande uniformité dans ses caractères essentiels, et répond de la même manière aux mêmes influences de milieu, quelle que soit la race ou la couleur, sous les tropiques comme dans les zones tempérées. Il faut seulement reculer assez loin, placer le point d'observation assez haut, pour que le jeu bigarré des détails ne nous cache plus les grands mouvements des masses. Alors les "modi" de l'humanité qui, toujours en mouvement, lutte, souffre et travaille, disparaissent à nos yeux et sa "substance" éternellement la même et éternellement renouvelée, immuable dans le changement même, nous découvre ses lois monotones."—Oppenheimer, *L'Etat, ses origines, son évolution et son avenir,* pp. 44-45, as quoted by Leclercq, *Leçons de droit naturel,* I, 29.

[32] Leclercq, *op. cit.,* pp. 28-29.

tion of nature, should disclose the fundamental laws governing the correct order of human society. This order is exactly what is intended by the term *Natural Law.*

In their search for truth, scientists generally proceed according to two methods, either *a priori*, i.e., from cause to effect, or *a posteriori*, i.e., from effect to cause. Only the latter, obviously, is immediately helpful in a study of human nature. In the sense used here, *nature* signifies the "inner principle from which the faculties or appetites of a thing spring."[33] But not even the natural faculties or appetites of a thing are immediately attainable by the human mind. Knowledge of a nature will, then, have to begin with the ends or achievements of these faculties, which objects are clearly perceived by the senses.

A few examples will illustrate the general principle that the end of a thing defines its nature. The reverse is also true. Once the nature of a thing is sufficiently ascertained, it is possible to predict the necessary ends of its faculties and operations. To grasp the nature of a pen, one looks to the product of its operation, i.e., writing. In ordinary parlance, it is very common to define a thing by what it does. A vehicle, one would say, is something used to transport people or merchandise over land from place to place. In the order of animated beings, the nature of a tree is understood in part by the fact that it sends forth leaves and blossoms, and further by its shedding of a seed for the growth of other trees. To know what an animal is, similarly, it will be necessary to study its habits, its manner of living.[34]

If man wishes to understand his nature, therefore, he must study, by direct observation or reflection, the natural functions of his faculties, vegetative, sensitive and rational. No different

---

[33] Cronin, *The Science of Ethics*, I, 130. In the same manner, Webster defines nature: "That which is the source or essence of life; creative force; the powers that produce existing phenomena."

[34] The structure of a being, while it contributes some information, does not give as penetrating a knowledge of it as do its proper operations. "Un insecte et un autre insecte diffèrent par les pattes, les élytres ou les mandibules; mais Henri Fabre entend mieux les connaître en observant leurs gîtes, leur alimentation, leurs accouplements, leurs mues, leurs métamorphoses."—Sertillanges, *La philosophie des lois*, pp. 32-33.

in this respect than other beings, man has his own natural stock of tools adapted to various ends.[35] He has, for instance, teeth to chew, hands to grasp, digestive organs to sustain his life, and reproductive organs to maintain the human species. He is also endowed with faculties of speech and thought, characteristics of men alone. All this apparatus is open to common everyday experience and inspection. And the same remark applies to the natural instincts and tendencies which suggest the use of these faculties. There is a whole gamut of drives and needs in man, of which he is well aware. Hunger, thirst, sexual instinct, desire for knowledge, need of society and religious tendencies are but a few of the fundamental inclinations which reveal the intimate nature of man.

A distinction should be made immediately between the fundamental inclinations of men, both such as are given by nature, and such as are created by men. The latter may be natural, but not in the sense intended here, as "given by nature." Thus, for example, the inclination to drink alcoholic beverages and to eat cooked food may be called natural, but not in the same sense as the fundamentally natural inclination to eat and drink. One can live without alcohol and *cooked* food; one cannot do so without food and drink.[36]

SECTION 2. ESSENCE OF THE NATURAL LAW

One should ask at this point: What is the relation between these natural instincts and the idea of Law, of Natural Law? The relation is the product of man's rationality.[37] Although non-rational

[35] Man can, however, fabricate or invent other tools, besides his natural ones, to achieve various human ends.

[36] Cf. Cronin, *The Science of Ethics*, I, 164.

[37] "When I said a moment ago that the natural law of all beings existing in nature is the proper way in which, by reason of their specific nature and specific ends, they *should* achieve fullness of being in their behaviour, this very word *should* had only a metaphysical meaning (as we say that a good or a normal eye 'should' be able to read letters on a blackboard from a given distance). The same word *should* starts to have a *moral* meaning, that is, to imply moral obligation, when we pass the threshold of the world of free agents. Natural law for man is *moral* law.

beings do not know their proper meaning, they also are endowed with natural inclinations, which drive them in a determined manner to the development and perfection corresponding to their nature. Man, on the other hand, is not only aware of the presence of these natural tendencies, but his reasoning powers enable him to grasp their purpose, i.e., to realize the content of goodness and perfection inherent in them. The good constitutes in effect, the motivating force behind all human actions: it is, therefore, the end of his whole nature. As St. Thomas says, "omne agens agit propter finem, qui habet rationem boni,"[38] i.e., every agent has a determined goal for his actions, and if he selects that goal it is due to the attraction it exercises upon him as a result of its desirability as something good. The basic rule, consequently, that man applies to himself is: "Do good and avoid evil,"[39] and its social counterpart: "Render to everyone his due," i.e., the good that is due to him as a man.

In that light, man sees the objects or ends of these natural appetites as so many means of attaining his total good, his full development as a human being. As a result, these instincts take on the character of reasonableness. They are no longer mere dynamism or impulsion, but ideology, maxims, practical judgments, rational principles of action.[40] The imperative of doing good and avoiding evil is thus detailed into so many derived rules of conduct, i.e., various precepts of the Natural Law.[41]

because man obeys or disobeys it freely, not necessarily, and because human behaviour pertains to a particular privileged order which is irreducible to the general order of the cosmos and tends to a final end superior to the immanent common good of the cosmos."—Maritain, *Man and the State* (Chicago: The University of Chicago Press, 1951), p. 87.

[38] *Summa Theologiae*, Ia IIae, q.94,a.2.

[39] It must be understood that the good referred to in the first natural precept is the good that is related to the specific rational nature. There are, as a result, other possible formulations of the first principle, such as "*medium tenere*," "*rectitudinem servare*,"—St. Thomas, *Scriptum Super Sententiis Magistri Petri Lombardi* (4 vols., ed. N. F. Moos, Paris: P. Lethielleux, 1947), d.37,q.1,q.4,ad 2um.

[40] Sertillanges, *op. cit.*, p. 34.

[41] "In other words, man's basic and prime duty is to become (in fact, actually, fully, completely) what he is (in idea, potentially, germinally,

It is interesting to note, with Maritain, the double process by which man's reason perceives the moral value of his natural instincts. The more perfect, of course, involves a serious reflection and study proper to the science of Ethics or Law. It is with this science of the Natural Law that this work is primarily, although not exclusively, concerned. As the noted author shows, however, there seems to be another manner of perceiving these realities, an instinctive and non-conceptual grasp of the order inherent in the natural tendencies in man. This conception would explain how a child, or an adult not given over to reflection, could arrive at certain conclusions similar, in some cases, to those of educated moralists. The possibility of error is, of course, much greater.[42]

Such an interpretation of the Natural Law would also explain why men of violently opposed ideologies and religious backgrounds could come to a practical agreement on a list of natural human Rights.

> "This fact merely proves that systems of moral philosophy are the product of intellectual reflection on ethical data that precede and control them and reveal a very complicated type of geology of the conscience, in which the natural work of spontaneous, pre-scientific, and pre-philosophical reason is at every moment conditioned by the acquisitions, the servitudes, the structure and evolution of the social group." [43]

In this regard also one wonders if St. Thomas did not have in mind this notion of instinctive Natural Law (knowledge by inclination) when he stated:

> "Omnia illa ad quae homo habet naturalem inclinationem, ratio *naturaliter* apprehendit ut bona, et per consequens ut opere prosequenda; et contraria eorum, ut mala et vitanda." [44]

---

essentially) through the consistent and persistent use of his reason and free will in the light and direction of his natural inclinations."—Rommen, *The Natural Law*, p. 178, n.2.

[42] Cf. *Neuf leçons sur les notions premières de la philosophie morale* (Paris: Pierre Téqui, 1951), pp. 47-57.

[43] Maritain, *Man and the State*, p. 80.

[44] *Summa Theologiae*, IaIIae,q.94,a.2; see also a.3: ". . . ut scilicet

Thus the specific precepts of the Natural Law (*"propria principia"*) would not really be conclusions from the first principle, but would be conceived as such, in the practical realm, in a manner similar to the conclusions deduced from the first principle in the speculative order (*"quasi conclusiones principiorum communium"*).[45] Likewise, these same specific precepts, when known in an instinctive manner, would properly belong to the Natural Law; when known in a reflective and deductive manner by philosophers who reflect upon them, they would pertain to the *ius gentium.*[46] This is Maritain's explanation of the somewhat obscure terminology used by Saint Thomas.[47]

The present writer is not in a position to judge this subtle distinction, although it does seem plausible to him as a historical solution. He does not feel compelled, however, to adopt the terminology of St. Thomas, and will continue to speak of the Natural Law even when treating of further conclusions rationally deduced from principles. If a principle pertains to the Natural Law, there seems to be no reason why a conclusion virtually contained in it and logically deduced from it should not also pertain to the Natural Law. From the natural principle that men must live in society, for example, one logically derives the principle that some form of authoritative government is necessary to rule over them; this also belongs to the Natural Law.

To summarize the notions already acquired, one could say that the essence of the Natural Law comprises two distinct elements. The first, its *naturalness*, derives from the natural functions of man's faculties and the natural inclinations to exercise them. The second element, the element of *law*, owes its origin to the light of reason, which grasps the relation between these faculties and instincts and the human acts of men. Reason commands that in

---

omnia illa facienda vel vitanda pertineant ad praecepta legis naturae, quae ratio practica *naturaliter* apprehendit esse bona humana."—Italics in both quotations are the writer's.

[45] *Ibid.,* a.4.

[46] Cf. IaIae,q.95,a.4.

[47] *Man and the State,* p.91,n.11; p.98,n.13.

all actions men conform to the order indicated by their natural instincts.[48]

SECTION 3.

APPLICATION OF THE NATURAL LAW CRITERION

A. Natural and Unnatural Use of a Faculty

It will prove useful to give some instances of the application of the primary criterion of Law as outlined above. "The first and most obvious instance of the use of the primary criterion is the case known as the natural and unnatural use of a faculty." [49] For purposes of greater clarity, the explanation will concern the unnatural use of a faculty, which takes place when the latter is used in such a way that it frustrates the realization of its own end. Misuse of a faculty implies two things, i.e., actual use and perverse use. One should therefore avoid confusing the unnatural use of a faculty or appetite and the simple non-use of it. Because of the complexity of man's faculties and inclinations, it is impossible for him to exercise all of them to the same degree, and it is perfectly legitimate, in certain cases, to sacrifice the use of one in order to attain more easily the good of another.[50]

Saint Thomas classified the natural inclinations of man into three categories, i.e., according to whether they pertain to him as

---

[48] Cf. Farrell, *The Natural Moral Law According to Saint Thomas and Suarez* (Ditchling: St. Dominic's Press, 1930), p. 97.

[49] Cronin, *The Science of Ethics*, I, 133. This author's exposition will be closely followed in the subsequent pages.

[50] ". . . we are not to conclude that each man is under an obligation to secure the ends of all the appetites. For, first, no man could possibly attain them all; and, secondly, the interests arising out of one appetite are often at variance with those of another, and, therefore, both cannot be attained. Thus marriage and a soldier's duty are in some circumstances quite incompatible. It is for Reason to determine in each case what is best for each one to do, the general principle of Reason being that each man should attain some of the ends which belong to the life and perfection of the individual whilst the duty of attaining what appertains to the life and perfection of the race devolves, not on each individual but on the race, such and so many individuals only being required to share the burden who are necessary for the attainment of the required end."—Cronin, *The Science of Ethics*, I, 646.

an individual substance, as an animal, or as a rational being.[51] Examples taken from each class will illustrate how the criterion of Natural Law is applied to social life. It is asserted, first, that as a substance man tends naturally to preserve his existence, to resist all elements which would destroy his life. All the powers of man have a specific purpose or object as their end, and through this end they collaborate in the attainment of a fuller development of being in the individual person who possesses them. One concludes, therefore, that suicide, which is a voluntary act directly aimed at destroying one's own being, is forbidden by the Natural Law.

> "There could be no more direct or unequivocal violation of nature than this. To use a power and to use it for the accomplishment of what is most directly opposed to its own natural end is the most complete perversion that is possible of nature's purpose and aims." [52]

Applying this point to the social field, to man's relations with other human beings, it confirms the assertion often made that a man has a natural Right to live, because this Right is based on the natural drive of his whole being. Only for some higher motive, therefore, could the ruler of a community pass a sentence of death over an individual, v.g., for the very preservation of the society over which he presides. Man is indeed a member of society and as such finds himself, in some way, in relation to it as the part is to the whole. Because of this, his good is subordinated to the good of the whole, and must sometimes be sacrificed to it. There are exceptions to this rule, however, inasmuch as the spiritual side of his being renders man superior to society.[52a]

One might wonder if, under a similar consideration of higher motives, a person could not legitimately contemplate suicide. His-

[51] *Summa Theologiae,* IaIIae,q.94,a.2.

[52] Cronin, *op. cit.,* II, 53. The author points out that although the man committing suicide does so because of some good he expects to derive therefrom, he nevertheless cheats himself of the possibility of achieving his natural good.

[52a] For a complete survey of this, see chapter III, Article II, The Common Good and Human Liberty, pp. 119-130.

tory tells us of many instances, especially in the Far East, where suicide took on the form of a supreme act of worship and dedication to God. Leaving aside such mistaken notions, could not a philosopher explain the reasonableness of suicide when it became necessary for the common good of society? One thinks, for instance, of the case of a prisoner of war who knows that he cannot go through cruel torture without revealing valuable military secrets. May this man commit suicide for the sake of safeguarding these secrets and thus averting certain calamities from befalling his country?

Christian ethics instinctively repels the thought, because it constitutes a direct contravention of all the natural tendencies of life. From a rational point of view, one could argue for the negative in the following manner. Society, it is true, has a Right to the co-operation of its citizens in the keeping of valuable secrets. This is a good end, a just end, and society may command that it be pursued, but only with equally good and just means, i.e., those which are in full accord with the fundamental inclinations of human nature. The real common good, the one that should and will prevail in the long run of civilization, is that which redounds to the dignity of the person. It might be immediately useful to society that a person commit suicide, as in the case described above; it certainly cannot contribute to the true and lasting common good. If society cannot exist except at the expense of the person, it has lost its purpose and thereby the Right to exist.

The objection that immediately comes to mind suggests that in going to war man sacrifices his life (and sometimes almost as readily as if he were committing suicide) for the sake of his country. The precise flaw in the argument lies in the word "almost." When risking his life for a superior motive, man rises above his natural instincts of self-preservation, because he realizes that the end which they indicate is not the ultimate end of the human person. But he does not thereby directly contravene the order which these natural inclinations make known to him, an order which the Author of human nature has therein inscribed and which man is not at liberty to violate.[53]

---

[53] The difficult question of the morality of suicide is lengthily studied by Leclercq in his *Leçons de droit naturel,* IV, P.I, 12-60, especially 53-60.

The second class of inclinations common to man concerns him as an animal. Under this class St. Thomas placed the sex organs and the instinct which inclines the male and the female to unite in sexual intercourse: thus nature provides for procreation and thereby the preservation of the human species.[54] No special powers of observation are needed to discern that the natural function of the sex organs in man and woman have the child as their end or object. Through some accidental cause, called sterility, the exercise of these faculties does not always produce a child, but this does not change the natural order of things. No one will contest that eating is ordained to nourish the body, even though some form of sickness in the stomach may prevent it from achieving this purpose.[55] The Natural Law thus commands that persons using the sex faculties respect the intrinsic order inherent in them.[56]

There are, of course, numerous social consequences resulting

[54] Note the proper end of the sex functions: the preservation of the species. This suggests that they need not be used by all men at all times. It may even prove laudable, in order to devote more time and energy to the pursuit of higher ideals, to abstain entirely from their use, provided the human race is in no danger of extinction.

[55] "The natural law does not merely command us to avoid whatever may harm ourselves, our fellows, or society; it commands us rather to observe the natural order of things imposed upon us by the Author of nature as means to the end, lest such harm ensue. Indeed, we are not bound by the natural law to attain certain ends so much as we are bound by it to observe the order of nature as the means to their attainment. Since, therefore, it is not so much the immediate and proximate duty of man to attain the various ends of his nature as it is to observe the order itself which has been established for the sake of such ends, a person may not consider himself no longer bound to observe the natural order simply because some end is in a given case accidentally unattainable. God does not, by means of the natural law, impose obligations upon human nature through the individuals who share in it; He rather imposes obligations upon individual men through their human nature itself."—Rommen, *The Natural Law,* p.181,n.7.

[56] Everybody sees the obvious conclusion: the exclusion of artificial birth control. So-called natural birth control, either through abstention or through the use of the rhythm method, respects the natural functions of the sex organs and therefore cannot be censured under this consideration, if at all.

from the physical union of the two sexes. It will suffice to mention only a few. The most obvious, of course, is the rearing of children. If men in general need society, how much more does the child, who must pass from the state of complete helplessness to one of adult maturity? The normal means of upbringing and education are provided by both the mother and the father who surround the product of their mutual love with tender affection and solicitude. This is the natural basis for the establishment, by means of an abiding marriage, of the group called the family.[57] This group, because it is a natural one, has in turn the Right to educate the child according to its own standards of belief and culture, provided that there ensues no violation of either the Rights of the child or of the State.[58]

On the negative side, the Natural Law affecting the physical union of the sexes would more directly forbid, for instance, that society pass laws requiring all married people to practice artificial birth control, and punishing all offenders who procreate children. The writer is unaware of any law having precisely that effect. Not so chimerical is the case of state-sanctioned diffusion of artificial birth-control methods. It is one thing to permit a lesser evil (v.g., prostitution) to avoid a greater one, and another thing to positively encourage evil. However acute be the problem of overpopulation, an unnatural attempt to solve it cannot be the answer. Nature has its ways, in time, to punish its violators. One recalls the emperors of decadent Rome pleading with its dissolute people

---

[57] There is another purpose for marriage, indicated in the physical and psychological make-up of the two sexes which complement each other: it usually comes under the heading of mutual support of husband and wife. Hence, even where it is known that the primary end of a physical union is unattainable, the physical union of the sexes and the pleasures ensuing are still quite lawful; always under the supposition that the natural order is faithfully observed.

[58] State aid to education must, therefore, always remain what it purports to be, namely, *aid* and not complete control. Only when the parents are found substantially deficient in this task may the State take over completely, but, again, only to protect the Rights of the child. Obviously this question, as all the questions mentioned in this section, would require much more detailed explanation; but that is properly the scope of more specialized studies.

to bear more children in the interest and for the protection of Roman society.

In this respect, it might not be useless to ask if the State can positively command the use of the sexual faculties. Such a law, obviously, could not be directly enforced without invading the privacy of citizens, but there are examples in history which show that an indirect enforcement was attempted. What of the justice, for instance, of the *lex Iulia* (18 B.C.), which disqualified an unmarried person from receiving benefits under a will unless he was related to the testator within the sixth degree, or unless he subsequently married within 100 days of the reading of the will? Similarly, under the *lex Poppaea* (9 A.D.), childless persons could inherit only half of the benefits left by a testator who was not a near relative.[59]

Granted that the legislator's intentions were good, and that the population of Rome was badly decimated, was the endeavor to force citizens to sexual intercourse just? Even excluding the obvious injustice done to those persons who could not marry or could not physically procreate children because of infertility or other accidental causes, one would have to score, it seems, such forms of legislation as violations of the human person's dignity and, therefore, as thorough injustice. The end does not justify the means. Although man's sex faculties properly belong to the animal side of his nature, he must use them as a human being, i.e., as a free and intelligent being who chooses this form, among others, of expressing his love for his life partner or of assuaging his passions. Intercourse between humans is not a merely biological function subject to the dictates of the State. In this regard, the State is limited to educative and persuasive measures, to which citizens are bound to comply if the need becomes truly great.

Not so easy to solve from a purely rational point of view is the problem of eugenic sterilization. Its proponents argue that it is necessary for the common good of society that mentally diseased persons be sterilized; this averts the great social danger accruing from the increase of idiots in society. The writer does

[59] Cf. Leage, *Roman Private Law*, 2.ed. by C. H. Ziegler (London: Macmillan & Co., Ltd., Reprint, 1951), p. 262.

not wish to linger on the scientific value of such a program which, incidentally, is far from being established. A noted zoologist, Professor Theodosius Dobzhansky, gives this conclusion from a table of the progress of selection against a recessive gene:

> "This shows the immense difficulty which would be encountered by selection against rare recessive defects or diseases in man, contemplated by some eugenical programs. Taking into consideration that the length of a human generation is at present some 25 years, such eugenical measures would have very little effect in a predictable future."[60]

Eugenic sterilization must be distinguished from therapeutic sterilization. The latter consists in a mutilation of the sex organs which, in their very existence, endanger the health of the whole organism. Individual parts of the body do not have an autonomy of their own: their value is assessed by their contribution to the health of the whole. Whenever they do not pursue this normal course (in their organic constitution—not in the free use made of them) they may and should be amputated, when possible.

The theory of eugenic sterilization establishes the same parallel between the person and society. It fails to see that the human person is not an integral part of society, except as a member thereof with social functions and activity and, therefore, does not have the same relationship to it that the bodily organs have to the body.[60a] A person is a whole in itself, independently of society.

---

[60] *Evolution, Genetics and Man* (New York: John Wiley & Sons, Inc.; London: Chapman & Hall, Ltd., 1955), p. 121.—For a good scientific evaluation of the claims of sterilization proponents, see also Lehane, *The Morality of American Civil Legislation Concerning Eugenical Sterilization,* The Catholic University of America Studies in Sacred Theology, 1st series, n.83 (Washington, D.C.: The Catholic University of America Press, 1944), pp. 38-62.

[60a] In his allocution of May 14, 1956, on corneal transplantation to a group of doctors, Pope Pius XII distinguishes very clearly between the physical organism of man and the moral organism of humanity and society. "L'organisme physique de l'homme est un tout quant à l'être; les membres sont des parties unies et reliées entre elles *quant à l'être physique* même; ils sont tellement absorbés par le tout, qu'ils ne possèdent aucune indépendance, ils n'existent que pour l'organisme total et n'ont d'autre fin que la sienne.

Prior to his participation in organized society (in the logical order) man possesses all the Rights of a free and intelligent being, including that of bodily integrity. Only when he abdicates this prerogative of humanity by a criminal act, can these Rights be directly attacked by the State. And even then such an attack will be permissible only in the event that it is absolutely required for the common good. Any other direct assault on a person's body constitutes a violation of the Rights of integrity which he possesses. Such an assertion does not contradict the general notion that society has a Right to command the active and intelligent co-operation of its members for the furtherance of the common good. It merely limits its use of means to those that are consonant with human dignity.[61]

There are, finally, inclinations resulting from the specifically rational features of man. In consequence of his intellect, man has an insatiable appetite for knowledge and desire to communicate this knowledge to others: hence, on both counts, there exists the necessity of living in society. Man has other needs, physical as well as intellectual, that urge him to unite in society with his fellowmen. That the instinct of sociability is properly of a rational origin can be explained by the fact that only men are able to grasp the notion of common good as the cornerstone of society.[62] Man's need of society is not based entirely, therefore, on his ma-

---

Il en va tout autrement pour l'organisme moral qu'est l'humanité. Celui-ci ne constitue un tout que *quant à l'agir et à la finalité*; les individus, en tant que membres de cet organisme ne sont que des parties fonctionnelles; le 'tout' ne peut donc poser à leur égard que des exigences concernant l'ordre de l'action. Quant à leur être physique les individus ne sont en aucune façon dépendants les uns des autres ni de l'humanité. . . ."—*Acta Apostolicae Sedis, Commentarium Officiale* (Romae, 1909-1929; Civitate Vaticana, 1929—), XLVIII (1956), 461; italics are the writer's.

[61] For a further discussion on the morality of eugenic legislation, see Lehane, *op. cit.*, pp. 63-95; Blais, *Les tendances eugénistes au Canada* (Montréal: L'Institut Familial, 1942), pp. 110-120; Leclercq, *Leçons de droit naturel,* I, 44-55.

[62] On this point, see Kreilkamp, *The Metaphysical Foundations of Thomistic Jurisprudence,* The Catholic University of America Philosophical Studies, Vol. LIII (Washington, D.C.: The Catholic University of America Press, 1939), pp. 71-73.

terial deficiencies. One should say that he depends upon society above all for help in developing the work of reason and virtue which is characteristic of his being. The need for character training and education requires the constant co-operation of other men: "society is thus indispensable to the accomplishment of human dignity."[63] It is not difficult to deduce important consequences from the instinct of sociability. The most obvious, one which has been asserted often in this work, is the need of an authoritative government capable of enacting laws for a more orderly pursuit of the common good.

> "For there are many different means by which the end of any society may be attained and a ruling authority is required to fix upon one definite set of means and to insist on these being followed. Without such authority the citizens who compose the State would be a rabble not a society. Without authority there could be no *conspiratio virium*, no common endeavour, no order, no progress. On the contrary, without authority the community would be constituted of opposing units, actuated by opposing forces, and the result would be the speedy disintegration of society."[64]

B. The Natural Order of Ends

It has been shown, so far, that the Natural Law commands respect for the essential order indicated between the faculties of man and their proper ends. There now arises a more intricate problem touching on the relation of these ends among themselves, and also their relation to the total good of man.[66] There is, in fact, a natural order suggested between the various faculties by the greater or lesser breadth of object subtended by each one of them.[67] The vegetative faculties have a much narrower scope than the intel-

[63] Maritain, *The Person and the Common Good*, p. 35.

[64] Cronin, *The Science of Ethics*, II, 516.

[66] It is taken for granted here that man may lawfully use and even destroy material things and non-rational beings provided this is truly useful to his development.

[67] "Genera vero potentiarum animae distinguuntur secundum objecta: quanto enim potentia est altior tanto respicit universalius objectum."—St. Thomas, *Summa Theologiae*, Ia,q.78,a.1; cited by Cronin, *op. cit.*, I, 137.

lectual faculties. There follows the natural subordination of the inferior appetites to the superior ones. In turn, all the particular faculties are subordinated to the integration of the whole man.[68] With this in mind, a person finds himself in a position to solve some of the more difficult conflicts of duties and Rights that arise in the field of Ethics and Law.[69]

Here are a few illustrations. The drinking of intoxicating liquor is not in itself unlawful: it provides legitimate pleasure and satisfaction to the vegetative and sensitive faculties. Such drinking can, however, become morally wrong when, solely for the sake of this momentary enjoyment, it induces loss of reasoning in man. In the last sentence, the restrictive clause is most important. To provoke unconsciousness, in fact, either naturally through sleep or violently through alcohol or drugs, can become perfectly lawful if it is necessary for the well-being of the whole man. It would not be unnatural, furthermore, to suspend the operation of the intellect in order to remove some slight bodily disfigurement. Although the body is inferior to the mind, its perfection nevertheless has a value of its own, not simply as a means to an end, but as a particular end itself. As Cronin says, "a temporary suspension of a higher faculty in order to secure a permanent good in a lower one is quite in accordance with the order and requirements of nature." [70]

To explain the prevalence, in certain concrete situations, of the lower ends over the higher ones, it is necessary to look to the principle of the integration of man's self. Because the lower ends do contribute something valuable to this integration, they must

[68] "As, therefore, in any organism each part has its own end distinct from that of other parts, yet serves certain other parts, and as the end of each part is subordinated to the end of the whole, so every faculty in us has its own end or object, but is subordinate to the wider faculty which contains it and to the whole organism, since the end of the whole organism includes the end of each part. From these relations we derive the laws of organisms. And these laws give rise to moral precepts."—Cronin, *op. cit.*, I, 138.

[69] One should note immediately, however, that the possession of certain general principles does not preclude the possibility of error or imprudence in the application thereof.

[70] *Op. cit.*, I, 139.

prevail in some circumstances; only when their prevalence would frustrate the higher ends must they be sacrificed.

> "A mother must nurse her child whose health is in serious danger and give up attending divine service, although the end of devotion to the child ranks in itself lower than that of devotion to the Creator; in the process of realization, however, in the particular circumstances described, the end of devotion to the child's well-being prevails, since the end of its preservation is in danger of being frustrated, whereas the end of devotion to the Creator can still be attained. On the other hand, devotion to the Creator holds its rank as the ultimate end when man's relation to Him is directly in question, because there is danger of man's ultimate end in Him being altogether frustrated; therefore the mother must not deny her religious belief in case of religious persecution, even though her life and thus the child's future are threatened." [71]

The social implications of the order of ends in man are obvious. The Rights of man as a man cannot be completely overshadowed by the exigencies of the common good of society. The common good is, indeed, an end in itself, and as such extremely desirable. Because it is "common," it prevails, in certain of its aspects, over the good of the individual man, who is related to society as a part to the whole.[72] On the other hand, because the common good cannot be understood except in relation to man whom it purports to serve, it must never take on the quality of an absolute and ultimate end in itself, i.e., irrespective of the individual members of that society.[73]

---

[71] Messner, *Social Ethics,* p. 26.

[72] The restriction implied in "in certain of its aspects" wants to make provision for the purely spiritual side of man, whose end, even as regards the individual man, is superior to the common good of society. See *above,* p. 58, and especially *below,* Ch. III, Art. II, The Common Good and Human Liberty, pp. 119-131.

[73] "Certains biens sont en eux-mêmes des fins infravalentes qui peuvent et doivent être employées comme des moyens, mais jamais comme de *simples* moyens. Le bien commun de la communauté civile est même une *fin ultime,*—dans un ordre donné, non absolument parlant; c'est une fin

The problem envisaged here is an intricate one, especially in its more concrete applications. A person's Right to live, for example, is very precious: desirable in itself, it is also a means to the attainment of even higher ends, material, intellectual and spiritual. It may be sacrificed, however, when the common good of the society, nay the very existence of that society, is threatened to such an extent that it demands such a sacrifice. Here the good of the individual falls before the good of the many. One sees, nevertheless, that rulers must be circumspect in the application of this rule, lest they have innumerable crimes on their hands.[74]

In concluding this section, one may serviceably furnish a definition of the Natural Law. In its scientific stage of development,[75] the Natural Law could be defined as a body of rational dictates resulting from man's grasp of the necessary order implied in the relation of his faculties or appetites to their natural ends, and in the coordinate or subordinate relation of these ends to the integration of the whole self.[76]

SECTION 4.
DERIVATIVE CRITERIANS OF LAW

It would be quite presumptuous to believe that the application of the primary criterion always yields conclusive evidence in regard to the problems of Law.

> "For sometimes, on account of the complicated reasoning involved, we are not able merely by considering the ends or

---

infravalente qui, dans l'ordre temporel ou terrestre, a valeur de fin ultime, de fin à laquelle tout le reste est ordonné; ce n'est pas la fin ultime pure et simple de la vie humaine, cette fin ultime pure et simple est supra-temporelle." —Maritain, *Neuf Leçons sur les notions premières de la philosophie morale,* p. 81.

[74] Reference is made particularly to a declaration of war involving the lives of countless citizens. Only when the agencies of government have moral certitude that this action is necessary for the preservation of its society can they presume to endanger the lives of its soldiers. All other means of settling disputes must have been previously exhausted.

[75] Cf. *above,* pp. 55-56, for the instinctive Natural Law.

[76] For other similar definitions, see Rommen, *The Natural Law,* pp. 181-182.

objects of our faculties to say whether a particular act is natural or unnatural, good or bad. In such cases we can often have recourse to other criteria which tell us indirectly whether an act is natural or unnatural, from a consideration, namely, of some necessary consequence or concomitant of natural or unnatural action—something which a natural act either involves or excludes." [77]

Not all of the secondary criteria afford the same strength of argument. Some of them, because of their intimate connection with the primary criterion, give the same degree of certainty as the latter. The conclusiveness of others ranges from a low degree of certainty to a high degree of probability. Be that as it may, they deserve some consideration because of their helpfulness in the solution of some abstruse problems of Natural Law.

A. Criterion of "General Injury With General Observance"

The value of this criterion stems from the metaphysical principle that nature never tends to its own destruction. Whatever be its nature, a being always tends to its development and perfection, either instinctively or deliberately.[78] Any general course of conduct, therefore, that works destruction in a general way cannot be in accord with nature. Applied to men, one would say that any course of conduct which, if generally observed, would prove injurious to the human race would sin against the nature of man, against the Natural Law. It is important to note the emphasis placed on the word "general." A particular action, because of the various accidents and circumstances pertaining to it, may be truly evil in itself and yet engender happy consequences. But if in all circumstances evil consequences result from a certain kind of action practiced at large, it is reasonable to conclude that the evil

[77] Cronin, *The Science of Ethics,* I, 140. Much of the following discussion on the derivative criteria is taken from this author. Although the latter is primarily concerned with moral *actions,* it will not be difficult to make the transition to the *laws* which command these actions.

[78] "Omne agens agit propter finem, qui habet rationem boni."—St. Thomas, *Summa Theologiae,* IaIIae,q.94,a.2. The destruction of a being may be "natural" in the sense that it is caused by other forces of nature, certainly not by the very nature of the being itself.

involved must be attributed to the essence of the action, and not to the circumstances.[79]

Because of the metaphysical foundation of this criterion, it will be advantageous to outline the conditions under which it is operative. First, the evil effects must spring from the act itself, and not from the intervention of the free will of certain agents. One could not argue, for instance, against the institution of private property because of the abusive exploitations of certain capitalists. Secondly, the evil consequences must not result from a by-product of the act. If the State, for example, were to oblige all women to work in factories, one could not conclude that the ensuing bad effects were attributable to factory work for women, but rather to the fact that there are no women left to care for the children and the homes. Finally, one must ascertain that excess has not become the contributing factor in the evil results. It would be ridiculous to assert that eating is unhealthy because one dies of starvation due to the too little amount of food consumed. Cronin summarizes the three conditions thus:

> "The general condition of application of the present criterion is that any evil consequences which serve as the criterion of the inherent evil of an act must be such as spring from the act itself specifically and necessarily, and not as a result of some adjunct to or circumstance of the act.[80]

A final note on this criterion remains to be stated. Stress should be laid on the fact that it manifests but does not constitute the evil character of an action or law. The evil consequences of an action which is raised to a general line of conduct merely indicate that the action is unnatural in itself, i.e., contrary to the natural

---

[79] "We should remark, however, that "injury" is a surer criterion of evil than "benefit" is of good; it is evident that nature reacts more surely and more promptly on the unnatural than it responds to the natural. A little poison will injure a man, whereas much good food may not increase his health. And hence we prefer to give as our expression of this present criterion the negative formula that 'What brings injury to the race when raised to a general line of conduct is bad'."—Cronin, *The Science of Ethics,* I, 142.

[80] *Op. cit.,* I, 143.

ends of the faculties or appetites in man. The primary criterion may or may not have yielded sufficient evidence to the mind. If it did, the derivative criterion will corroborate its findings. If not, this derivative criterion will furnish us with an indication, sometimes certain, that the act is unnatural, and that a closer inspection of the appetites of man may, some day, disclose that fact beyond any reasonable doubt.

A very important conclusion follows logically from the preceding remark. The act which, if raised to a general line of conduct, would prove injurious to the race is always evil in itself regardless of the good or evil consequences that flow from it in a particular situation. Take the example of artificial birth control already banned by the primary criterion. Sometimes the participants in this act benefit physically and financially from the limitation of children.[81] The fact that, if practiced on a general scale, it will gradually bring about the extinction of the human race does not make it evil, but simply manifests that it is such. Artificial birth control is not reprehensible *because* it is widespread and thus works destruction; but the evil consequences of this general course of conduct constitute one of the reasons (i.e., besides the primary criterion) why we *know* that every act of artificially controlling birth is unnatural, and therefore evil in itself.

One might argue that if all men followed the so-called natural method of birth control, this too would bring about the extinction of the human race; and therefore, natural birth control is also outlawed under this consideration. In answer to this objection, it should be noted first that although this method cannot be termed intrinsically evil (because it effects no direct violation of the natural order of the sex act), it does not automatically escape all possible censure. To enter marriage with the decided intention of practicing the rhythm method throughout conjugal life constitutes at least an indirect contravention of the primary purpose of marriage. To enjoy the pleasures of marriage without accepting its inherent responsibilities is not worthy of human beings. Because this method is not intrinsically evil, however, serious

[81] The writer wishes to point out that they might have achieved the same happy results through natural methods.

reasons of a hygienic and economic nature can legitimate its use. Here is precisely where the State can intervene, with proper housing projects and family allowances, to provide for the normal and healthy expansion of family life.

It is possible that some readers will find the exposition of this derivative criterion somewhat related to the theory of Utilitarianism. To avoid too close an association between the two doctrines, it seems pertinent to submit the following remarks. The criterion of "general injury with general observance" does not constitute but only manifests morality and is therefore only a derivative criterion. Utilitarians, on the contrary, insist that the well-being of the individual or of the race is the final natural end of good action and therefore its sole criterion.

> ". . . utilitarians believe that if a particular act itself brings unhappiness to the race, it is bad. We claim that if *an act should necessarily injure the race on being raised to a general line of conduct it must be bad.* These points of difference are essential and render the two theories not only distinct but radically opposed." [82]

B. Criterion of "Common Human Convictions"

The validity of the distinction between good and evil, between the just and unjust, has been upheld for centuries by men of all races and creeds. There must be a cogent reason for such a belief. There must be a reason, for example, why the human race has felt the necessity of the institution of marriage (although not necessarily monogamous) rather than any form of promiscuous relationship between the sexes. The simple answer suggests itself: it is because men have, through the ages, delved quite deeply into their own nature and realized, perhaps after other solutions had been attempted, that only marriage satisfied the needs of the respective sexes and the exigencies of society. The endless experience of history has taught many a lesson concerning the nature of men.

---

[82] Cronin, *op. cit.*, p. 148 (italics are the author's). The present writer regrets not being able to give a complete exposition and criticism of Utilitarianism. See the excellent coverage of Cronin, *op. cit.*, pp. 318-371; Del Vecchio, *Philosophy of Law*, pp. 426-430.

This fact is recognized by most modern legislators who accept the proven formulas of ancient systems of Law in their dealings with human problems.

The criterion of "common human convictions," although a highly useful one, is not the ultimate criterion of Law and morality: it rests upon the primary criterion of the ends of human nature and human society. Its particular value lies in its presentation of ready-made answers to problems which are not easily solved by recourse to the primary criterion, i.e., by reasoning from man's natural appetites.

> "We may or may not be able to apply the primary criterion in a particular case; but, if we can find a conviction upon any point from which mankind has never receded, we may trust to that conviction as a criterion of what is natural to man and apply it as a substitute for the primary criterion." [83]

Again it is necessary to show the distinction between this derivative criterion and the positivists' doctrine of public opinion. The latter argues that constant public opinion is the only rule of action, and it may vary according to time and country.[84] One of the difficulties attached to this theory is that public opinion is not always constant. To say that it is the opinion of the majority cannot always satisfy the consciences of the remaining percentage of the population. One accepts that normal issues will be settled by the vote of the majority. Some of these, indeed, are relatively indifferent, like the election of one man or another to an office. Others may be of greater importance (even some elections, v.g., when Communists seek office), and this points out the necessity of educating citizens in the fundamental notions of justice. In

[83] Cronin, *The Science of Ethics,* p. 154. The author also points out (p. 155, note) that, if the convictions were strengthened with reasons, then these reasons themselves would serve as the criterion: they might in fact prove to be an expression of the primary criterion.

[84] "Le Droit naturel absolu est une chimère. . . . Dans un pays donné, à une époque donnée, le Droit est donc l'ensemble des règles de conduite sociale que la majorité des hommes de ce pays et de cette époque estiment justes et socialement utiles."—Jése, *Les principes généraux du droit administratif,* p. iv (quoted by Leclercq, *Leçons de droit naturel,* I, 27).

this basic matter of what is just or unjust, the majority is not right simply because it is the majority. Very often, at the source of public opinion, one finds a leader or a group of leaders who have succeeded in enlisting a great many followers. Their great number does not guarantee the validity of the opinion they support, sometimes unthinkingly.[85] Before public opinion can compare with the criterion of "common human convictions," it must pass the scrutiny of centuries and survive the criticisms of systems of Law other than that of one country alone.

SECTION 5.
ULTIMATE SOURCE OF OBLIGATION OF THE NATURAL LAW

The reader may have been surprised, in perusing this exposition of the Natural Law by a Catholic writer, to see no explicit mention of the Eternal Law of God. The writer avows that he has consciously avoided such references, and for a definite reason. In the order of priority of human knowledge, the created precedes the Uncreated; the perception of the order of nature precedes the knowledge of a Supreme Cause of this order. In philosophy, the original process is always the same: from the effects which immediately manifest themselves to him, man rises to the cause of these effects. The writer hastens to emphasize that there are other means of knowledge available to man, namely, Revelation. The latter is of a higher order, the order of Faith. It is not opposed to reason, but aids and supplements it in its deficiencies. The Christian philosopher may have supernatural certainty (through Faith) on particular points of Law and Morals, but he should be very diligent, as a philosopher, to ascertain these truths through

---

[85] "L'opinion publique n'est pas souveraine; et pour mettre à néant cette souveraineté usurpée, il suffit de suivre sa genèse. Comment se forme l'opinion publique? Pas plus que les données de la prétendue conscience sociale ou de la masse des consciences individuelles, elle n'est un phénomène spontané. C'est l'opinion des meneurs et des entraîneurs; ce n'est qu'une opinion individuelle qui a fait boule de neige; elle n'a pas plus de valeur lorsqu'elle a recueilli des millions d'adhésions qu'au temps où elle était isolée; elle s'est accrue en puissance et en rayonnement, elle n'a pas grandi d'un pouce en valeur morale et en vérité."—Renard, *Le Droit, la Justice et la Volonté,* pp. 84-85.

purely rational methods. The writer holds, however, that the Natural Law studied on a philosophical level alone, cannot give a full explanation of man's destiny because, as he believes, man's end is not simply of a natural order, but really of a supernatural order. But since the latter does not destroy the former, a purely philosophical study of the Natural Law, besides finding acceptance in the minds of non-believers, has decided merits of its own.[86]

> ". . . though ontologically the eternal law is prior to and is the ground of the natural law, yet we are to conceive the natural law as logically prior in regard to us—that is, as coming first in the order of our knowledge. For just as it is from the existence of the finite world that we come to know of God's existence who is first cause of all, so also it is from the existence of the natural law of the universe that we establish Divine Providence and the existence of the eternal law. The natural law, since it exists in creatures, is an effect; and, therefore, it presupposes another law above itself from which it springs." [87]

These remarks show the foundation for making the Natural Law the primary criterion of Law and morality; that is, in regard to men, it is the proximate primary criterion. Because of man's immediate knowledge of his nature, of the order inherent in his natural faculties and appetites, he is conscious of his obligation to observe the precepts thereby translated to him. The proximate reason why man is obliged to follow the precepts of the Natural Law is that his reason tells him that otherwise he will frustrate the demands of his being. There is no choice possible from a moral approach: he must be rational, he must be a man.

A proximate criterion does not exclude an ultimate criterion. In freely accepting the order implied in his nature, man makes an act of autonomy; but he can never escape the fact that it is a created autonomy.[88] Man does not create the natural order: he

---

[86] For a thorough discussion of this delicate question, see Leclercq, *Leçons de droit naturel*, I, pp. 73-87.

[87] Cronin, *The Science of Ethics*, I, 643-644.

[88] "Nous maintenons, nous, l'ordre normal des choses. Il y a une nature humaine procédant de Dieu et comportant de par Dieu un dynamisme

sees it and applies it. To use a comparison, the contractor does not create the blueprint: he accepts it from the architect and builds accordingly, following the order suggested in it. In much the same way does the Natural Law depend on the Eternal Law of God.[89] Like all artists at work, God fashioned the world according to a preconceived idea already existing in Him. His Divine Providence, similarly, governs all acts and movements according to an eternal order of things always present in His Wisdom. This is what is called the Eternal Law, the ultimate criterion of Law, and the ultimate source of obligation of the Natural Law.[90]

From these considerations, one may draw the conclusion that subordinate legislators are subject to the supreme Master of the universe. If their laws are to conform to the dictates of right reason, they must be in accord with the supreme law of reason found in God. Any human law which contradicts the order of nature imprinted in man by God cannot be sustained as a true law. Although human positive law sometimes *permits* that which is contrary to the Eternal law, this is due to the natural limitations of an inferior rule of action. It cannot hope to encompass as large a field as a superior rule. This does not imply that human positive law

---

propre qui a le caractère d'une loi. L'homme en l'acceptant librement fait acte d'autonomie créée, en raison de quoi la loi naturelle qui le concerne se rattache à la loi éternelle."—Sertillanges, *La philosophie des lois*, pp. 24-25.

[89] ". . . il faut observer que la nature humaine est une nature raisonnable; que sa loi immanente est donc de sa part un objet de réflexion et ainsi d'acceptation ou de rejet. En l'acceptant, l'homme se la donne pour ainsi dire à lui-même, ainsi que le voulait Kant. L'erreur de Kant dans sa fameuse théorie de l'autonomie morale de l'homme n'était pas là. Elle était en ce que ce philosophe refusait de fonder en nature, et ainsi de faire remonter à Dieu, cette loi que l'homme s'impose à lui-même. L'homme ne relevait que de soi. Il était son propre Dieu, et il n'y avait pas de nature humaine."—*Ibid.*, p. 24.

[90] Cf. St. Thomas, *Summa Theologiae*, IaIIae,q.91,a.1; q.93,a.1.—It must be noted that in proper parlance there is no "preconception" in God, and also no distinction between God's essence and His Wisdom. To God, all things are present, and His action in the world is eternal. By analogy, nevertheless, it is legitimate to assimilate God's work to that of an artist, as Saint Thomas himself does.

does not derive from the Eternal Law nor that it is contrary to the Natural Law, but simply that it does not equal the latter in its scope.[91]

Recourse to the Eternal Law as the ultimate source of obligation of the Natural Law is not without practical utility. However strong be the dictates of natural right reason, they sometimes need the reinforcement suggested by the fact that it is God, the Master, who commands the observance of the Natural Law. This explains why adherence to the latter has been most strong, according to history, in times where knowledge and love of God has been uppermost in the minds and hearts of men.

Article III: Content of the Natural Law

That there is such a thing as a content of the Natural Law should to some extent appear evident to the reader of the preceding article. The principles of doing good and avoiding evil, of rendering to each person his due, are not the only principles governing human activity and Law. As a matter of fact, there is much truth to the statement of Maritain, namely, that these principles are the preamble to the Natural Law itself.[92] A preamble is an introduction: it indicates what is to be looked for in the text of a constitution, for instance, and what is to be used as the method of investigation. In a similar manner, the preamble to the Natural Law points out the necessity for man to seek the good in his every action and, in his relations with other men, to respect their good as something due to them as his equals.

Jurists are eminently practical men: they deal with laws in

[91] Cf. St. Thomas, *Summa Theologiae,* IaIIae,q.93,a.3. ". . . hoc ipsum quod lex humana *non se intromittat* de his quae dirigere non potest, ex ordine legis aeternae provenit. Secus autem esset si *approbaret* ea quae lex aeterna reprobat. Unde ex hoc non habetur quod lex humana non derivetur a lege aeterna, sed quod non perfecte eam assequi possit."—*Ibid.,* ad 3um (italics are the writer's). This particular problem will return in Chapter IV, which will deal with possible conflicts between the Natural and positive laws. Cf., v.g., pp. 139ff.

[92] Cf. *Les droits de l'homme et la loi naturelle* (Paris: Hartmann, 1947), p. 65.

their concrete application to individual cases. Because of their specialization, some of them show little patience for abstract thinking which has no direct and immediate relation to the case at hand. As it was explained above,[93] this attitude denotes a faulty understanding of the role of Natural Law in a juridical system. The Natural Law does not solve cases, it offers principles of solution. It does not pretend to replace positive law: it only wants to inspire and to orient it with the given rules of human nature.[94] This last remark does not imply that the formulas and principles of the Natural Law are empty, devoid of material content. Without having the form of a detailed code of laws regulating man's every action in the social sphere, the Natural Law offers certain clear-cut directions that he must take and certain limits which he must not exceed.

SECTION 1.
OBJECTIVE CONTENT

At this point it seems necessary to examine briefly one school of thought which, if closely pressed, leads to a denial of any objective or material content of the Natural Law. This view, proper to the modern idealistic school, has lately been restated by Professor Di Robilant in his study of the implementation of the Natural Law in the Canon Law of the Catholic Church.[95]

One could, it seems, summarize the author's interpretation of the Natural Law in the following manner.[96] Since human nature

[93] Cf. p. 46.

[94] Cf. Renard, *Le Droit, l'Ordre et la Raison,* pp. 121-122; 134-140, passim.

[95] *Significato del diritto naturale nell'ordinamento canonico,* Torino: G. Giappichelli, 1954. The book concentrates mostly on criticizing the views of the traditional Natural Law school as they are expressed by representative authors of the last century, i.e., those to whom canonists refer most often in matters involving the Natural Law. The present writer can only hope, in this terse analysis, to comment on the more salient points of doctrine expressed by the author, in order to clarify the issue at hand.

[96] As far as the writer can ascertain, Di Robilant has only three paragraphs (pp. 201, 202) in which he discusses his own opinion for itself. The latter can, however, be extracted from his criticism of the other theories.

does not exist for men except in the minds of individual men who think about it, an appeal to the Natural Law (the law of human nature) cannot be conceived in any other way than as an appeal to the individual man's reason.[97] The individual's reasoning is, on the other hand, conditioned by his own personal views in religion, philosophy, politics, sociology and other empirical sciences. His Natural Law solutions will, therefore, take on the color of these convictions and simply represent what, in the particular circumstances, he believes to be the ideal solution to the problem at hand, never excluding a better solution to be reached at a later date.[98] One must draw the logical conclusion, always according to Di Robilant, that it is inane to assert that *the* Natural Law commands a certain course of action; it is rather the individual legislator who, conscious of his duty to serve the common good, commands that course of action, because he believes it to be the best possible solution to a particular problem.[99]

---

[97] "Una realtà che non sia quella da noi conosciuta, per noi non esiste; una realtà che condizioni la nostra conoscenza non può essere che quella che noi conosciamo."—*Op. cit.*, p. 96. "Razionalè mi pare venga allora implicitamente a significare, nel sistema del Taparelli, e come si vedrà, anche nei sistemi degli altri giusnaturalisti, conforme alle esigenze speculative di ciascun pensatore che proceda coerentemente dai primi principi. L'elemento personale che ogni uomo pone nella ricerca, elemento che non comporta peraltro il polverizzarsi della verità nel sogettivismo, si trova implicitamente racchiuso nel termine 'razionale', dato che i primi principi sono puramente formali, così come la coerenza nel trarne sviluppi, e senza un apporto specifico del singolo uomo non dànno ancora luogo ad un pensiero."—*Ibid.*, p. 28.

[98] "In realtà poi, dall'esame della dottrina dei giusnaturalisti, è emerso che il diritto naturale finisce per identificarsi con il complesso delle soluzioni che ciascuno di essi ritiene le migliori per i singoli problemi della convivenza sociale, soluzioni informate a principi di varia natura: religiosi, filosofici, politici, sociali, nonchè a criteri di mera opportunità basati sulla semplice empiria. Ora, se è così, alla radice delle norme del diritto naturale stanno sempre il giudizio e la decisione del singolo che le proclama tali, giudizio e decisione che riflettono l'intelligenza e la cultura di lui e il clima storico e sociale in cui egli si trova a vivere."—*Op. cit.*, p. 194.

[99] "Il diritto naturale diviene invece un momento di tutto o di una parte del diritto positivo, e non più un diritto autonomo affiancato al secondo; diviene cioè il momento della razionalità, della maggior conformità delle

To do full justice to this view of the Natural Law, one would have to criticize at great length the epistemological foundation on which it rests. The scope of this work permits only certain remarks which, it seems, should be sufficient to contest the validity of the opinion, without giving the impression that the assertions advanced are entirely false.[100]

It is quite true to say that the Natural Law does not exist as *Law* except when formulated by reason; and since this is a law applying to men in concrete cases, one refers to the reason of individual man. It should be carefully noted, on the other hand, that the Natural Law is not only Law, but it is also *Nature*. To be sure, this nature will not be known to men except by their reasoning powers. But there is a valid distinction between reality as such and reality as perceived by man. In the very statement that reality exists only in the mind of men, there is implied the reality of the mind itself. How could the mind operate in the first place if it had to wait for its perception of itself to exist as a reality?

Admittedly, this is common sense philosophy. Just as the mind exists before it reflects upon its activity, so also do the data of human nature exist in concrete reality before being formulated by human reason as so many dictates of the Natural Law.[101] This

---

soluzioni prescelte (riferita ad altre possibili soluzioni) alle esigenze della ragione. Il dire, perciò, come accade spesso da parte dei canonisti, che una determinata norma è 'di diritto naturale' . . . non significa altro se non che tale norma è giudicata da colui che lo afferma 'giusta', 'razionale', non negabile senza contraddire alle esigenze della sua ragione, alle *sue* esigenze speculative prese nella loro complessità, quelle esigenze secondo le quali il singolo impegnato nella *sua* ricerca *esprime* cio che è nel profondo, esprimere che non è mai adeguazione ma appunto sempre et solamente *espressione.*" —*Op. cit.*, p. 200; italics are the author's.

[100] The writer has already alluded to the epistemological problem in the first article of this chapter. See pp. 48-50. See also Gilson, *Réalisme thomiste et critique de la connaissance*, Paris: Librairie Philosophique J. Vrin, 1947.

[101] In criticizing Renard's appeal to the Natural Law to justify a rule of conduct in a particular situation, Di Robilant (*op. cit.*, p. 74) considers it as a mere appeal to a person's own reasoning, there being no written Code of Natural Law whose pages could be thumbed in search of the practical solution. But then, why not apply his doctrine to the perusing of a book

does not mean that individuals will always have the same views in regard to all points of Natural Law. Some of the data of human nature are so readily observable to man that they require little or no discretion on the part of the individual judgment before being accepted as a part of the Natural Law. Not so easily formulated are those principles, for instance, which deal with the complex notes of man's social nature. It is precisely in those more involved problems that a person's upbringing and beliefs are liable to play a decisive role. The writer believes, however, that a constant return to experience, to the experimental sciences of sociology, anthropology and ethnology, will enable men to separate the facts from the beliefs. With the precious observations and criticisms of others who have also studied the particular problem, they will eventually, in many cases at least, arrive at a solution certainly indicated by nature.[102]

To adopt one illustration, it is readily observable that the natural tendencies of man direct him towards self-preservation. This he accepts as the law of his nature and only under stress of disordered passions or intentions will he be tempted to violate it. Transferred to the social sphere of activity, this law commands respect for the lives of others. But there are many complications that may enter the picture. What is to be done with a notorious criminal who threatens the peace and security of other citizens? The very general principle is clear: the part is inferior to the

---

of positive law? The laws therein collected do not exist unless they are made the object of an individual's creative and original thinking, a thinking deeply affected by the individual's culture and moral background. An appeal to positive law is also, therefore, even when the solution is clearly indicated in that law, only an appeal to the best possible solution invented by the lawyer or judge handling the case involved.—It is needless to say that such a position would meet with very little favor in juristic circles.

[102] "La science du droit naturel cherche à déterminer les exigences du droit naturel. Comme toutes les sciences qui reposent sur la connaissance de la nature, elle est difficile et ne peut arriver à une connaissance parfaite de son objet que par un travail long et minutieux. Dans les données du droit naturel, il en est qui apparaissent à première vue; d'autres sont plus cachées. Mieux on connaîtra les exigences de la nature sociale de l'homme, et mieux on connaîtra celles du droit naturel."—Leclercq, *Leçons de droit naturel,* I, 55.

whole and, as such, can be sacrificed for the good of the whole, if need be. The problem is thereby not solved but shifted to the determination of "need." In exterminating "inferior races," Hitler believed in the overriding value of purity of the "whole." One must therefore go one step further and ask: In what way, however, is man a part of society? Is he an integral part of society as the hand is an integral part of the body? The answer is clearly negative: society is not a physical and substantial organism.

> "The human person is engaged in its entirety as a part of political society, but not by reason of everything that is in it and everything that belongs to it. By reason of other things which are in the person, it is also in its entirety above political society." [103]

The good of life, of temporal existence, is not an absolute good. It is inferior in quality to the moral and spiritual values and even to the salvation of the community. It remains, nevertheless, one of the most important pre-requisites for human development: it is thus a Right which can be forfeited only when the individual inflicts damage to the common good through an irrational use of his faculties. Because of this relation to the person, it cannot be subordinated to the good of society in such a way that considerations of mere social utility would suffice to legitimate its sacrifice.

One comes to the conclusion that the life of a criminal may be taken from him only when this is necessary for the very preservation of society. Is it ever absolutely necessary? Is life-imprisonment sufficient, in modern society, to deter other members from crime? The answer to these questions is not obvious, as is witnessed by the opposition to capital punishment.[104] Here there is room for discussion because the desired conclusion is far removed from the general principle. Individual authors who study this question are apt to be swayed by their temperamental inclinations to leniency

---

[103] Maritain, *The Person and the Common Good,* p. 51. As previously noted, this matter will receive extensive treatment in Chapter III, Article II. Cf. pp. 119-130. See also *above,* p. 63, n. 60a.

[104] Cf., v.g., Leclercq, *Leçons de droit naturel,* Vol. IV: *Les droits et devoirs individuels,* Ière Partie: *Vie, Disposition de soi,* pp. 70-98.

or severity. But if they carefully analyze the reasons for capital punishment and the data of experience, taking into account the multiple causes of delinquency, they will perhaps arrive, some day, at a conclusion as to the necessity or non-necessity of such punishment for the good of society. What will society do in the meantime? The arguments in favor of capital punishment give sufficient assurance (only moral certitude is possible) that the Natural Law would not thereby be violated. What future investigations conducted by jurists will disclose can only be a matter of conjecture.

It is at this point that Di Robilant's "best possible solution" receives its valid application. Some conclusions may or may not pertain to the Natural Law; or, in some cases, the connection between the principles and conclusions may not appear convincing. In the case just discussed, capital punishment may or may not be demanded or even permitted by the Natural Law. If it is demanded, the present studies of human nature and human society do not seem to have clearly revealed this to men. In such situations, the legislator has a choice: the realm of positive law has perhaps been reached.

SECTION 2.
GENERAL AND SPECIFIC PRECEPTS

The foregoing discussion gives rise to many considerations of interest to the jurist. The first conclusion to be drawn is that, while some of the rules of the Natural Law are most general, others are quite specific. The natural Right to one's life, admitted universally, finds very practical applications in the daily social picture. Legislators and jurists consider it in practice as something much more concrete than an empty formula of words. The same observation applies to other basic Rights attached to the dignity of the person, such as the Rights to one's honor and reputation, to the enjoyment of one's property, to freedom of religion and expression. A cursory and objective study of man's nature reveals these fundamental Rights quite readily. There is no lack of precision, no vagueness at this level. It is only when the particular objects of these individual Rights are confronted with the similar Rights of others and of society that great difficulties arise. Deductive reasoning no longer suffices here. It is necessary to go down into the field of social relations to discover under concrete circumstances what social conditions are necessary for the full development of man in society. A long-standing tradition of thought and experience has disclosed many of the natural exigencies of social life; others have yet to be learned.[105] In the first instance, one will surrender to the facts of human nature, to the Natural Law. In the second, one will continue the study of human nature and meanwhile adopt the best possible solution known at that time.[106]

It remains quite true that the Natural Law contains more general than particular rules. Dealing with nature and natural inclinations, it does not immediately supply a norm for the concrete situations created by man's resourcefulness. As one author aptly puts it, it does not regulate the "buying and selling of shares on the stock-exchange" or the "ordination of a cleric outside his home diocese." [107] But since when is the term *Law* reserved to those norms that are immediately applicable? The position of the Natural Law in relation to the positive laws may be compared to the Constitution of the United States in relation to the laws of the various States. Even in the latter the degree of immediate practical application differs considerably from one law to the other. The tendency to completely separate the Natural Law from the bodies of positive laws distorts the picture of human activity. Just as it is impossible to say that in a particular action man

[105] ". . . with regard to the basic *ontological* element it implies, natural law is coextensive with the whole field of natural moral regulations, the whole field of natural morality. Not only the primary and fundamental regulations but the slightest regulations of natural ethics mean conformity to natural law—say, natural obligations or rights of which we perhaps have now no idea, and of which men will become aware in a distant future. An angel who knew the human essence in his angelic manner and all the possible existential situations of man would know natural law in the infinity of its extension. But we do not. Though the Eighteenth Century theoreticians believed they did."—Maritain, *Man and the State*, p. 89.

[106] Cf. Leclercq, "Note sur la position actuelle du droit naturel," *Revue néo-scolastique de philosophie* (Louvain: Institut Supérieur de Philosophie), XLI (1938), pp. 267-278.

[107] Kuttner, "Natural Law and Canon Law," *University of Notre Dame Natural Law Institute Proceedings*, III (1949), 102.

disregards his destiny as a human being, so also is it incorrect to say that the positive law governing this action is independent of the Natural Law. The former embodies the latter in the same manner as the operations of man embody his nature.

SECTION 3. KNOWLEDGE AND CERTAINTY OF THE NATURAL LAW

The progressive knowledge that men acquire of the Natural Law engenders at various levels varying degrees of certitude. To the constant factors readily accessible in the study of human nature in operation corresponds a high degree of certitude in the minds of those who advert to them. Because it is not always possible to ascertain the constancy of certain factors in the various operations of men, especially in society, the conclusions drawn from them do not always offer the same strength of argument. The degree of certitude attached, for instance, to the physical laws, such as the law of gravitation, is superior to that attached to the laws of economics, such as, for instance, the law of supply and demand. In the realm itself of physical laws some of them are more certain than others, v.g., the law of gravitation as opposed to the "laws" of evolution or genetics. So it is with the Natural Law. If experience teaches that certain social conditions are certainly and evidently necessary for the development of man, such as the institution of private property, then one will conclude that they are *demanded* by the Natural Law. Inasmuch as the findings of experience, in the present stage of human knowledge, are not always so conclusive, one might have to say that the Natural Law prescribes certain conditions as only *highly desirable*, rather than as absolutely required.[108]

---

[108] It is in this sense that one historian of St. Thomas suggests that be understood the famous distinction, classic among scholastics, between the primary and secondary precepts of the Natural Law. As a matter of fact it appears only in one of St. Thomas' original works, and a very early one at that (*In IV Sent.,* d.33,q.1,a.2). In a later attempt to explain the same question of polygamy versus the Natural Law, the author makes no mention of it (*Summa Contra Gentiles,* III, c.123-124). The fact that a pious but uncritical disciple utilized the passages of the *Sentences* in his *Supplementum* to the *Summa Theologiae* (q.65,a.1,c.& ad 1um,2um) explains

For that same reason, i.e., the uncertainty of some precepts of the Natural Law, it is not always possible to discern whether a particular law actually in effect receives its validity directly from the Natural Law or from the positive law itself. The entire system of laws, in other words, is composed of both natural laws and positive laws, and it is difficult in some concrete cases to ascertain where natural reason ends and where positive reason begins. Scientists encounter a similar difficulty in other fields of investigation. Zoologists and botanists readily accept the specific distinction between animals and plants (a distinction very useful to them, incidentally), but they cannot always discern with absolute certainty to what species belong the beings situated at the extremities of each order. Zoologists or botanists would not for that reason alone reject their respective sciences as useless. Nor should jurists reject the Natural Law because of the uncertainty of some of its more particular conclusions.

Because the Natural Law is discovered and manifested as the product of human reason, it cannot escape the general condition of trial and error to which all human knowledge is subject. Like all sciences studied by men, the science of the Natural Law advances by overcoming the ignorance of some and the errors of others. It would not be surprising if the primitive tribes did not have as penetrating an insight into human nature as that made possible today through greater intellectual and moral development. The worst aberrations in this field, even in modern times, do not prove anything against the Natural Law itself, not any more than errors of addition disprove the science of mathematics.[109]

---

but hardly justifies its general acceptance as the definite thought of St. Thomas in the matter.—Cf. Lottin, *Le droit naturel chez saint Thomas d'Aquin et ses prédécesseurs* (2. ed., Bruges, Belgique: Charles Beyaert, 1931), pp. 76-79; 102-103. See also Aubert, "Les citations de droit romain dans l'oeuvre de saint Thomas," *Revue de droit canonique*, V (1955), p. 158, n.17.

[109] "Natural law is an unwritten law. Man's knowledge of it has increased little by little as man's moral conscience has developed. The latter was at first in a twilight state. Anthropologists have taught us within what structures of tribal life and in the midst of what half-awakened magic it was primitively formed. This proves merely that the idea of natural law,

The science of the Natural Law could probably make great strides today if only the modern mind would apply to the study of human nature a scientific method equally as rigorous as that which is used in the study of physical nature. Considerations of a purely sentimental or utilitarian nature have no place in determining the necessary laws of human beings. The argument given in the case of therapeutic abortion, that the mother's life is more precious than the child's, is a good example of such loose and sentimental thinking. It is surely more correct to base a judgment on what is certain than on what is uncertain. On the one hand, there is the absolute certainty, offered by his natural inclinations of self-preservation, that every human being has a Right to live. The inability of the foetus to defend this Right does not argue against its possession of it. On the other hand, there is the more or less plausible surmise that the mother's life will prove more valuable to her family and to society. Nobody can be sure of that. Nobody knows for sure that the mother will not succumb to a heart attack upon leaving the hospital, or will not leave her children and run off with another man. No doubt, death in childbirth is a very sad incident, one in which the persons affected require sympathy and assistance on the part of others. These sentiments are genuinely human and worthy of men. Not so human is the sentiment according to which the murder of an innocent human being is directly perpetrated. Looking at the problem from the real point of view of human destiny, the Right of the unborn child to life seems, in a certain respect, more appreciable than the mother's. Life is a means of perfection. The mother has already benefited by some years in which she could achieve this, at least

at first immersed in rites and mythology, differentiated itself only slowly, as slowly even as the idea of nature; and that the knowledge men have had of the unwritten law has passed through more diverse forms and stages than certain philosophers or theologians have believed. The knowledge which our own conscience has of this law is doubtless itself still imperfect, and very likely it will continue to develop and to become more refined as long as humanity exists. Only when the Gospel has penetrated to the very depth of human substance will natural law appear in its flower and its perfection."—Maritain, *The Rights of Man and Natural Law* (London: Geoffrey Bles, The Centenary Press, 1944), pp. 36-37.

partially. The child must be given an equal chance to attain the grandeur possible to every human being.[110]

SECTION 4.

MEANING OF IMMUTABLE PRECEPTS

The traditional school of Natural Law has always proclaimed that its principles are, in themselves, absolutely immutable in time and space, i.e., they have been, are, and will be valid for all men of all centuries and nations. Even after the explanations given in this and the preceding articles, such a broad and sweeping statement requires a few elucidating remarks.

It should be noted, in the first place, that immutability and universal validity attach to these principles only in an objective sense. That is to say, whatever they be, by whomever they are known, if they are truly Natural principles, they are as immutable as are the basic tendencies and goals of human nature upon which they are founded. This does not mean that they will always be recognized and correctly interpreted as objective and immutable principles, especially (but not exclusively) in the initial instinctive phase of the Natural Law.[111]

In this respect the writer would like to point out what he thinks is a slight exaggeration on the part of certain authors. Rommen, for instance, states that the precept forbidding the killing of an innocent person shares very highly in the self-evidence and immutability of the first principles, i.e. of doing good and avoiding evil, of rendering to everyone his due.[112] He adds that "the killing of an innocent person has at all times been considered a crime."[113] Besides the well-known exception to this statement taken from the killing of old people to save them from suffering, it is doubtful if mankind has always understood the term "innocent" in the many and various shades of meaning now given to it. There seems to be a confusion here between objective and subjective immutability, one perhaps engendered by too great a

---

[110] Cf. Leclercq, *Leçons de droit naturel*, IV, 63.

[111] Cf. *above*, pp. 55-57.

[112] *The Natural Law*, p. 221.

[113] *Ibid.*, pp. 222-223.

desire to assert the self-evidence of the Natural Law; as if it were necessary for its validity that the full implications of at least its most obvious precepts be ascertained in all the stages of the intellectual development of men. One might be closer to the truth in affirming simply that even primitive people considered the killing of a man not as easily justifiable as the killing of an animal. Whatever be the actual knowledge of the Natural Law (and today civilized people do recognize as certainly pertaining to this Law the precept, among others, of not killing innocent persons), this does not affect its objective immutability.

A more specific understanding of the immutability of the Natural Law precepts might have to take into account the following observations. A precept dealing with the intrinsic order of a human faculty to its natural end admits of no exceptions in any sense. Thus, for instance, the natural ordination of the sex organs to procreation may never, under any consideration, be frustrated by a direct artificial or external obstacle. In the same manner, lying can never be permissible, because it clearly violates the intrinsic purpose of speech, which is to convey outwardly the convictions of the mind. In this respect, it is true to say that God, in His Wisdom, can no more change the Natural Law precepts than he can change the nature of a circle by making it square.

Looking now to the natural ends or goods which some particular principles of the Natural Law protect, one must realize that they do not in themselves embody the full and ultimate good of man. For that reason these principles of the Natural Law do not have the absolute range of validity possessed by the supreme principle of doing good and avoiding evil. In that sense, the particular good of human life, for example, may at times (in the manner explained above)[114] be limited by the similar good of others or subordinated to higher values expressed in the common good. Thus, while it is true to say that the inviolability of the human Right to life is immutable at the particular level of good for which it is formulated, it is not so absolute that it cannot yield to goods of a higher level. In other words, one must adapt these principles to the hierarchy of human ends.

---

[114] Cf. pp. 81-83.

SECTION 5.

APPLICATION OF THE NATURAL LAW

The writer has endeavored to show in this article that the Natural Law has much more to offer than the very general direction of doing good and avoiding evil, of rendering everyone his due. The natural good and just are spelled out in so many individual precepts, according to the various natural ends to which man tends. Most of these precepts are admittedly quite general, others are more particular, and others still are so particular that they need very little, if any, further determination to be applied to concrete situations. One should, however, be careful not to oversimplify matters to the point of thinking that the immediate norm of behavior derives rigorously as a conclusion from the major and minor premises. Such an interpretation would certainly confuse the particularization of precepts with the application of these same precepts to individual circumstances. It is this rigid syllogistic reasoning that Reinhold Niebuhr criticizes when he speaks of "the mistake of Catholic moral casuistry to derive relative moral judgments too simply from the pre-suppositions of its natural law . . ."[115]

Once the pertinent principles of Natural Law have been invoked, there remains the judicious task of applying them correctly to the situation at hand. This is a *prudential* task with which no grasp of the principles can dispense. Even the suppositions of the most detailed system of casuistry cannot cover every conceivable situation with its individuating aspects.

> "No amount of casuistic 'if's' could meet and be adequate to the contingent circumstances of conduct. There can be no universal file of proximate norms for behaviour. The proper precepts of individual actions are to be found in the particular precepts of prudence—not in the law, which, natural or hu-

[115] *The Nature and Destiny of Man* (New York, 1949), pp. 220-221, as quoted by De Koninck, "General Standards and Particular Situations in Relation to the Natural Law," *Proceedings of the American Catholic Philosophical Association* (Wash., D.C.: The Catholic University of America), XXIV (1950), 28. The latter article, of penetrating insight, is responsible for many of the considerations contained in this section.

man, retains a certain degree of generality. No law can be the particular premise of an operative syllogism in which one infers what is to be done *here* and *now*." [116]

Principles are, by their nature, rigid. Since they are so, they cannot always apply as such to cases to which normally, *in abstracto*, they were conceived to apply. That St. Thomas and his followers are aware of this is evidenced by the following oft-quoted text:

> "Thus it is right and true for all to act according to reason, and from this it follows, as a proper conclusion, that goods entrusted to another should be restored to their owner. Now this is true for the majority of cases. But it may happen in a particular case that it would be injurious, and therefore unreasonable, to restore goods held in trust; for instance, if they are claimed for the purpose of fighting against one's country. And this principle will be found to fail the more, according as we descend further towards the particular, e.g., if one were to say that goods held in trust should be restored with such and such a guarantee, or in such and such a way; because the greater the number of conditions added, the greater the number of ways in which the principle may fail, so that it be not right to restore or not to restore." [117]

St. Thomas understood well, then, the necessity of some intervening and immediately practical judgment as to the advisability of applying to a particular situation the rule which is normally applied to situations of this kind.[118] This is the judgment of prudence, a judgment which implies not only circumspection and foresightedness, but also and especially a "rectified appetite," i.e., a sincere desire to make sure that *here* and *now* the application of this or that law will really implement the cause of justice. In the example which St. Thomas uses of the goods held in trust, if

[116] De Koninck, "art. cit.," pp. 28-29; italics are the author's.

[117] *Summa Theologiae,* IaIIae,q.94,a.4,c. (Translated by Pegis, *Basic Writings of St. Thomas Aquinas*, New York: Random House, 1945).

[118] For an excellent documentation and summary of St. Thomas' views in the matter, see Deploige, *Le conflit de la morale et de la sociologie,* pp. 315-316.

the person who was normally bound to restore them lacked foresightedness or more especially if he cared little about the possible malicious use of these goods, his restoration of them, far from being a correct application of the Natural Law, would be a violation of it.[119]

The need of prudence, of careful discrimination, appears all the more evident in the application of more determinate principles. The particular conditions attached to the latter, conditions which the case at hand must fulfill before it can be regulated by these principles, render all the more mandatory a careful scrutiny and sympathetic analysis of the case in all its individuality.

> "This is true of natural law, but it is no less true of human law. The multiplication and refinement of particular rules provides no excuse for neglecting the irreducible peculiarity which no just law was ever meant to overlook. The application of any law must always be an act of prudence, which is 'circa singularia contingentia,' and whose judgment depends upon the condition of the appetite. No law could possibly render irrelevant either the knowledge of this contingency or the disposition of the appetite. To overlook these two factors would spell intolerable tyranny. Reality, in this order, is never simply rational." [120]

CONCLUSION

It appears from the foregoing considerations that the science of the Natural Law is by no means an easy one, especially when it deals with the complexities of social life. The present writer would not be honest with himself if he pretended otherwise. But since in the long run of things ideas do rule the world, it is important that even today, after thousands of years of social experimentation, they be correctly adjusted to the views of God manifested by the nature of human beings and the necessary institutions in and by which they live. Man can learn much through

---

[119] This important point is well brought out by De Koninck, "art. cit.," pp. 29-30.

[120] De Koninck, "art. cit.," p. 31.

the efforts of his own reason alone. It is a pity, however, that realizing the finiteness of his intellect, he does not always find it within himself to accept the additional instruction given by Divine Revelation and proposed in an infallible manner by the true Church of God.

CHAPTER THREE: POSITIVE LAW

Article I: Elaboration of Positive Law

SECTION 1.

GENERAL DEFINITION OF POSITIVE LAW

One could define positive law, the subject-matter of this third chapter, as "that system of juridical norms which gives form to and regulates in fact the life of a people at a particular period in history."[1] Adequate as a description of the role of positive law, this definition does not sufficiently distinguish its object from the Natural Law, which was treated at some length in the previous chapter. To accomplish this, it would have to qualify the juridical norms of positive laws as those norms which are the product of man's own activity. In contradistinction to the Natural Law, positive law is the creation of man.

It is pointless to insist on the existence of positive law. A brief examination of its *raison d'être* will, however, shed some light on its nature. In this respect, the superficial view might state simply that positive law concerns itself with the more concrete determination and application of general norms to individual situations. There is much truth to such an answer, but it does not fully justify the existence of positive law, nor does it express its main characteristic. One might, indeed, suggest that each man's prudential judgment would be as sufficient in the field of Law as in the field of individual morals. In the matter of temperance, for instance, the Natural (moral) Law prescribes that man partake of enough food to sustain himself. No particular determination of quantity is offered him: this is left to his discretion. Moral philosophers or theologians and casuists may offer valuable indications and guiding rules; they can never tell each man just how much bread he should eat, nor exactly how many packs of cigarettes he may or may not smoke.

[1] Del Vecchio, *Philosophy of Law*, p. 305.

Positive law goes further, and, in some instances, very much further. In extreme circumstances, v.g., in times of war, it will even establish ceiling prices on certain necessities or commodities, and control the rates of rents charged by landlords. This does not mean that prudence is outlawed: it always plays an important role in the judicious adaptation of law to situations.[2] The necessity of greater determination, sometimes minute, lies in the fact that positive law governs an entirely different realm of life, the social life, the order of Right. The judgment of one person does not suffice, because there is always more than one person involved. In the order of individual morals, the person concerned can be allowed to decide what is best (prudence does not, however, exclude good counsel) precisely because he alone will be affected by the consequences of his actions. Only he will suffer from an incorrect application of the Natural Law.[3] When morality enters the social field, its particular determinations cannot be left to the sometimes biased and prejudiced judgment of the individual. An objective and authoritative interpretation is needed to safeguard the true interests of all concerned. This is the object of positive law.

Positive law represents an attempt to establish what is Right, to make justice between two or more persons, when this has not been sufficiently expressed by the Natural Law. The just (object of justice) cannot be considered from the point of view of one person alone. It is entirely objective: Scholastics called it the "*medium rei*" as opposed to the "*medium rationis vel subiecti*" of individual morals.[4] In some cases, the just may be determined by the persons involved under a private pact or agreement. Buyer and seller may agree on the price of an article and thus decide on what is just between themselves alone: this is positive law

[2] See *above*, pp. 90-92.

[3] Cf. Bender, *Philosophia Iuris*, p. 196.

[4] As St. Thomas explains, the mean of every virtue is a rational mean. In opposition to justice whose mean is taken from objective fact, i.e., according to the relation of Right existing between two or more persons, the other moral virtues regulate and moderate the passions from the sole consideration of the individual himself. Cf. *Summa Theologiae*, IaIIae, q.64,a.2,c.;IIaIIae, q.58,a.10,c.

at its lowest level. Because most of these transactions have social overtones, at least insofar as disputes and discords may arise therefrom, the private regulations governing them are usually subordinated to the laws of society as a whole. This is positive law at its superior level. It springs from the will of the people which manifests itself through various fashions: either implicitly or by actions, thus giving rise to custom, or explicitly by direct legislation. In larger and better organized societies, the latter function usually devolves upon one or more representatives of the people, with infrequent recourse to the people in the matter of elections or plebiscites.[5]

SECTION 2.
FOUNDATION OF POSITIVE LAW

In his remarkable work on positive law, Gény asserts that the activity of the jurist swings constantly between two poles, which he calls the "*datum*" ("*le donné*") and the "*constructed*" ("*le construit*").[6] His work, on the one hand, consists purely and simply in examining social nature in itself and its implications. With the results of this investigation at hand, he will proceed to a personal and largely artificial construction of rules capable of implementing the requirements of the datum in everyday life. It would be incorrect to believe that the Natural Law, as it was explained in the previous chapter, is the sole foundation of positive law, at least in the sense that there is always a direct and immediate relation between the general rules of the former and their application in the latter. In other words, the datum upon which the positive jurist builds his construction of enactments or his interpretation of them is not entirely elaborated under the title of Natural Law. Gény, in fact, distinguished four levels of data which the jurist must investigate: natural or real, historical, rational and ideal.

---

[5] Cf. St. Thomas, *Summa Theologiae,* IIaIIae,q.57,a.2, as explained by Bender, *Philosophia Iuris,* pp. 198-208. The sources of positive law will be studied in further detail below.

[6] *Science et technique en droit privé positif* (4 vols., Vol. I, 2.ed., 1922, Vol. II, 2.ed., 1927, Vol. III, 1921, Vol. IV, 2.ed., 1930, Paris: Recueil Sirey), I, 96.

The "real datum" comprises those factual and natural conditions which serve as the very basis of any positive construction. These realities do not directly create the juridical rules, but they offer their general outline and indicate their necessary elements of content. To take an example, one that will be pursued throughout, the "real" datum discloses that there exist two different sexes which tend to join and to complement each other. The whole positive legislation on marriage will be built on this basic finding of nature.[7]

The "historical" datum is composed of all the legal achievements recorded in the history of mankind. It is certainly useful to the present-day jurist to scan the juridical accomplishments of the past, to study the various customs, written laws and jurisprudence of his ancestors. All the ancient systems of Law reveal themselves in their grandeur and weaknesses, thus pointing out the results to be expected from similar methods. Judged in this manner from a historical point of view, the union of the two sexes appears under the aspect of marriage, an institution closely regulated in its conditions and effects. Despite the accidental variations from one system to the next, it is always strictly controlled by some social authority.[8]

Under the caption of "rational" datum come all those precepts properly called Natural Law precepts. Reason dictates the laws of human conduct which can be extracted from man's nature and his necessary contact with the world. As the writer has often pointed out in the previous chapter, it is necessary to make a sharp distinction between those principles which natural reason clearly and surely postulates and those which it cannot establish except with the help of other considerations, which Gény relegates to the "ideal" datum. Thus the Natural Law certainly commands, in the matter of marriage, an abiding and permanent union as the regular means adapted to the foundation of a family worthy of social recognition. But to extend this precept to the point of

---

[7] Gény, *op. cit.*, I, n.167, pp. 371-376.

[8] Gény, *op. cit.*, I, n. 168, pp. 376-379.

requiring the absolute indissolubility of marriage seems, always according to Gény, to go beyond the realm of pure reason.[9]

The "ideal" datum embraces all those considerations of a physical, psychological, moral, religious, economic or political order which, without necessitating new principles of social conduct, nevertheless have much influence in suggesting the direction to be followed. These principles, or rather convictions, do not possess the absolute rational validity of the Natural Law precepts. Sometimes they pursue the indications of the Natural Law to points beyond the strict requirements of the latter. It is under this light, stated Gény, that must be interpreted the prohibitions against polygamy and divorce, as well as the other precisions and restrictions introduced in the institution of matrimony.[10]

It is easy to see, then, that the datum on which the jurist bases his construction and from which he draws his materials is not comprised solely of Natural Law principles. Some positive laws are an outgrowth of the Natural Law, in the sense that they regulate and protect the institutions which are vital to any form of social life. Those laws which deal with governmental authority serve as good examples. There are, on the other hand, countless positive laws, by far the most numerous, which have no direct connection with the Natural Law. All the prescriptions which govern matters of mere common utility in a particular society can be linked with the Natural Law only insofar as the latter requires that all laws procure the common good. One should be careful, therefore, not to extend the validity of such rules to all systems of positive law.

If positive law must conform to the Natural Law, this does not signify that in all its regulations it will completely meet the requirements of all the natural principles taken separately. Positive law deals with men in their concrete state of existence. It must

---

[9] *Op. cit.*, I, n. 169, pp. 380-384. The present writer is inclined to agree with the author up to a certain point. He believes that the absolute indissolubility of marriage, if not decisively commanded by the Natural Law, is certainly contained under it as something most highly desirable. Only reasons of a supernatural order could legitimate divorce, and then only under the direction of God or His representative on earth.

[10] *Op. cit.*, I, n. 170, pp. 384-389.

take into account all the circumstances in which they live. It must also pay special attention to their present moral standards and the immediate possibility of improving them. If a ruler desires beneficial results from his legislation, he must gear it to all these factual conditions of his subjects. Very often he will find himself forced to disregard or tolerate certain evils, which should eventually be uprooted. Some of his laws will even grant certain Rights to persons guilty of actions which are, in principle, injurious to society. Thus it is not unknown in the history of legal systems that concubines were protected by law against masculine abuses.[11]

If a positive law is not entirely in accordance with certain individual precepts of the Natural Law, one should not conclude that it is directly contrary to the Natural Law itself. To be sure, all positive legislation must attempt as exact an approximation of the Natural Law as possible, but it can do so only within the realm of its proper means, and also under the guidance of the primary principle of the social order, i.e., the common good. If in well defined circumstances of person, place and time, the enforcement of one particular natural precept would hinder the common good, it cannot and must not be commanded, and this by virtue of the Natural Law itself. A proverb finding application here says: the better is sometimes the enemy of the good.

Progress in positive law becomes, then, a gradual and judicious invasion of the field of social morals. It is not a purely mechanical process, i.e., one that would endeavor to adapt mechanically the Natural Law to concrete situations. Natural Law cannot always be molded into formulas of positive law. A great measure of common sense, tact and judgment is needed to determine the opportune moment for applying and enforcing certain principles of right reason.[12]

Another restriction in the attempt of positive law to approximate

---

[11] Cf. Leclercq, *Leçons de droit naturel,* III, 84-93.

[12] "Il n'y a pas de machinerie qui dispense le juriste de la charge et de la responsabilité personnelles qui lui incombent, de déterminer, à un moment donné, quelles conceptions morales sont bonnes à mettre en articles de loi ou en doctrine de droit positif. Ceci est un préjugé néfaste, avec lequel il faut en finir."—Renard, *Le Droit, la Justice, et la Volonté,* p. 111.

the Natural Law lies in its coercive mission. Positive law can prescribe usefully only that which it can physically enforce. It would be ridiculous to enact legislation which citizens could violate with impunity.[13] One might even venture to say that a society without laws would fare better than one with unenforced laws. This does not mean that the ideal solution is one where citizens obey laws only because of the physical force behind them. But humanity at large has not as yet made the full transition from obedience through fear to obedience through motives of a high moral quality alone. It is doubtful, moreover, if such a transition will ever be completely effected in this world. Imperfection is a necessary adjunct to creatures.

One would have to consider the extreme conservatism of positive law as another reason why it cannot hope to measure up to the full requirements of the Natural Law. And yet, this characteristic trait is itself again postulated by the common good. It is a well known fact that the formulas of positive law do not change in exact proportion to the times. Law abhors change.[14] Examples of this repugnance are plentiful. One could cite, for instance, the well known rule "*actori incumbit probatio,*" according to which the burden of proof falls upon the plaintiff precisely because he is in some way an innovator. Similarly, the possessor receives the protection of Law because of his presumably long-standing tenure. There is also the presumption that the legitimate government is that which is, in fact, already established in peaceful possession of power and accepted by the people. Revolutions are odious to law. As a last example, one might mention that the interpretation

---

[13] One might mention here the so-called *lex imperfecta* of the Romans. An example is the *lex Cincia* of about 200 B.C., which forbade gifts above a fixed amount except to certain relatives and other persons. This law merely forbade the gift, but did not void it. Its sole effect was to serve as a defense (*exceptio legis Cinciae*) to the donor against the donee claiming the gift. Cf. Buckland, *A Manual of Roman Private Law* (Cambridge: The University Press, 1953), p. 152.

[14] "Le droit n'est pas la vie; c'est tout au contraire le poids du passé appesanti sur le présent. Le droit est comme une liturgie qui canalise l'élan des générations nouvelles dans les formes où s'est solidifiée la pensée des générations disparues."—Renard, *Le Droit, la Justice et la Volonté,* p. 218.

of laws proceeds usually along a conservative pattern, according to the understanding of them that has been received as traditional in a given system. In other words, Law purifies progress by passing it through the sieve of the past, of that which is already acquired.[15] Unless this inflexibility is corrected by means of wider interpretation, construction or other legal devices, the juridical forms will sometimes and even very often clash with the exigencies of justice. Even if this were the case, one could still justify the obstinacy of positive law on the basis that legal instability is harmful to the common good. When laws change too often, citizens are apt to look upon them as fluctuating fantasies to which they should pay little attention. Engaged themselves in the anxiety-ridden struggles of a world in progress, they need the comforting anchorage offered by stable legislation and the customs that are formed in accordance with it. Only then can they know what to expect from the Law, and thus direct their actions accordingly.[16]

SECTION 3.
SOURCES OF POSITIVE LAW

The various forms of manifestation of positive law are usually grouped under the title of "sources." They are three in number, namely: custom, legislation and "jurisdiction." [17] The brief space allotted to each of these sources cannot possibly do justice to them. The controversies centering around them, especially as re-

---

[15] Renard, *loc. cit.*

[16] "Car une loi ne se fait pas pour un jour. Il y a au contraire intérêt à ce que son règne soit long, et le législateur doit bien se garder d'y apporter des modifications toutes les fois qu'il entrevoit quelque chose de meilleur à établir. On irait ainsi au désarroi de l'opinion et au désordre dans les affaires. Car en toutes choses et pour tous, la coutume est d'un grand apaisement et d'une grande force. Ce qui la heurte, fût-il peu important, semble aussitôt une chose grave. C'est pourquoi tout changement apporté à une loi, en tant qu'il rompt l'accoutumance, affaiblit le pouvoir légal. Il convient donc de n'y toucher qu'en vue d'un bien plus grand que n'est le détriment inévitable, comme de faire cesser une iniquité, de réaliser un progrès vraiment nécessaire, ou en tout cas d'une utilité reconnue de tous." —Sertillanges, *La Philosophie des lois*, p. 63.

[17] Following Del Vecchio, the writer thus refers to the contribution of judicial activity to Law. Cf. *Philosophy of Law*, p. 308.

gards their respective authority as expressions of Law, have not been definitely settled. Some remarks may prove helpful to a proper understanding of these sources.

A. Custom

Custom may be defined as unwritten Law which is introduced by a longstanding practice among the people. In the primitive stages of society, custom was the chief, if not the only, form of Law. Certain rules of social conduct, though not expressly imposed by any ruler, become rooted in the people as a result of their actual and almost instinctive observance of them. The material element of a constant and longstanding repetition of acts is accompanied with a sense of "obligatoriness." As Del Vecchio states:

> "In order that a *juridical* Custom arise, it is necessary that the repetition be strengthened by the persuasion that the behavior in question is *obligatory* so that *others can demand it*, and does not, therefore, depend upon mere subjective free choice."[18]

The duration of a custom is an important, though extrinsic, element because it manifests the uniformity or lack thereof in the repetition of acts. It thus establishes to a higher or lesser degree the validity of a practice as a binding norm upon all. It is, therefore, not surprising that various systems of Law give greater strength to immemorial customs.[19]

The writer is aware that he has just taken a stand regarding the juridical value of custom, in the sense that in fully organized societies such as they exist today it plays a role subsidiary to that of legislation. There seems to be a need for distinguishing the status of custom, in States where the people govern by themselves

[18] *Philosophy of Law,* p. 306 (italics are the author's).

[19] See, v.g., for the Catholic Church, *Codex Iuris Canonici Pii X Pontificis Maximi iussu digestus, Benedicti Papae XV auctoritate promulgatus, Praefatione, Fontium Annotatione et Indice Analytico-Alphabetico ab Emo Petro Card. Gasparri Auctus* (Romae: Typis Polyglottis Vaticanis, 1917, reimpressio, 1934), cc. 27, 30 (hereafter cited *C.I.C.* with appropriate canons); for English Law, Allen, *Law in the Making,* pp. 89-90.

directly, and in States where they delegate the exercise of this authority to representatives. It should be noted at the outset that this authority does not originate with the people themselves, not any more than it originates with one man alone. God is properly the sole origin of authority, as He is the origin of the sociability of man giving rise to it. The people merely detain it, regulating its exercise. Once they have handed over this exercise of authority to their delegates, they cannot refuse to obey the just dictates emanating from it. They cannot, moreover, rule in any way except by and through these representatives. In such circumstances, it would seem contradictory to assert that custom is on an equal and independent basis with the legislation of the actual detentors of power. There is no doubt that custom plays a decisive role in the formulation and interpretation of the articles of the constitution, which establish the Rights of the people in relation to the powers of their government. When the writer assigns an inferior position to custom, he refers only to those new customs which are created after the constitution has been drafted and accepted, and the reins of authority have been transmitted to elected representatives. One might go a step further and say that no custom is authoritative unless it is protected by at least the general approbation of the rulers. By this is meant that the rulers consent, at least implicitly, that all reasonable customs not conflicting with the established system of Law have the force of Law.[20]

One might argue that in democratic societies custom will always prevail in the long run, since the legislator "remains in power only insofar as his activity is sustained and, so to say, ratified by the social will, by the predominant persuasion." [21] This is a matter

[20] In Canon Law, this consent is called "legal" by some commentators. The fact that a custom fulfills the general requirements set down in the Code of Canon Law (cc.25-30) entitles it to full juridical status. On this point see Michiels, *Normae Generales Juris Canonici, Commentarius Libri I Codicis Juris Canonici* (2 vols., 2.ed., penitus retractata et notabiliter aucta, Parisiis, Tornaci, Romae: Desclée et Socii, 1949), II, 40-44. The writer realizes that the Church is not a democratic society. If Church Law was brought in here, it was only as an example of the consent required, and not as a justification of the reasoning advanced.

[21] Del Vecchio, *Philosophy of Law*, p. 317.

of fact, and points out the necessity of gearing legislation to the needs and capacities of the subjects. If it means that only those laws are valid which meet the immediate approval of the people, the door is opened to anarchy rather than Law. There should be room in any system for education through legislation. The social will is rather undefinable and sometimes inadequate in expressing the real common good. And what appears at times to be the social will is often only mass adherence to ideas and theories of individual demagogues and politicians.

These observations do not mean to minimize the extreme value of custom. The writer believes that custom should be sanctioned by all systems of positive law. Even the Catholic Church, which is essentially a monarchic society, has a high regard for it, to the point of allowing, in some instances, that it abrogate laws. To reject custom as a source of Law amounts to disregarding the tremendous psychological impact of tradition in the lives of the people. If people tend to act in conformity with the pattern of living set down by their ancestors, this does not merely manifest their acceptance of the law of the least resistance, but also their reverence for practices which have withstood the scrutiny of time. Custom does not involve a clear perceptual grasp of a situation nor an exact understanding of the principle applied in a given circumstance. But there is certainly a reason or motive behind the constant repetition of the same acts in similar cases, a reason which no legislation can afford to neglect. While legislators may and should be technically trained for their important work, they cannot abstract from the sound juridical principles that were applied in practice before being expounded as principles. It is furthermore to be noted that only custom can hope to cope quantitatively and even qualitatively with the juridical exigencies of daily life. This explains in part why jurisdiction (court justice) relies so heavily upon it in the solution of practical cases.[22]

B. Legislation

Legislation, in its present-day state, is a conscious and deliberate expression of Law emanating from certain well defined organs

[22] Michiels, *Normae Generales Juris Canonici,* II, 16-17.

of government. The emphasis on consciousness and deliberation is precisely what distinguishes it from custom. Del Vecchio states:

> "The law is, therefore, the solemn pronouncement of Law, its rational expression. Only in this form does the technical development of Law reach its greatest perfection." [23]

Even systems of Law which place great emphasis on custom and judicial precedent admit that legislation is the superior form of Law. An English author asserts:

> "The difference between custom and legislation as sources of law is manifest. The one grows out of practice, the other out of theory. The existence of the one is essentially *de facto*, of the other essentially *de jure*. Legislation is therefore the characteristic mark of mature legal systems, the final stage in the development of law-making expedients." [24]

Although not all systems can be classified as systems of Code Law, all of them tend, in modern society, to produce an increasingly larger amount of actual legislation. The reasons behind this tendency are interesting to the philosopher of Law.

The writer has already alluded to the fact that some customs do not favor the true common good. Probably reasonable and valid under circumstances of the past, they do not satisfy the requirements of the present. Some of them might even have been unreasonable from the start. Unanimity of the people is not always an infallible criterion of conduct. Actions express moral convictions, and history teaches that the latter have not always been beyond reproach. This explains in part why the legislature should intervene and abrogate certain customs.

If progress is to be achieved in positive law, and certain changes are periodically necessary, it should be the result of a general and long-range planning on the part of eminently qualified legislators. Although this postulate does not always correspond to reality, the chances that it may are greater than if the determination of positive law is committed into the hands of the people through custom

---

[23] *Philosophy of Law*, p. 309.

[24] Allen, *Law in the Making*, p. 238 (italics are the author's).

or of the judges through "jurisdiction." It seems easier to select a small group of jurists noted for their skill and integrity than to depend exclusively upon the same qualities in an immense body of lawyers and judges. Granted that social pressures are liable to affect the reasoning of both groups, they undoubtedly will have less influence on those who look to the future and lay down universal norms to be applied by others, than on those who have to decide concrete cases. Leaving too much leeway to the decision of individual judges seems to place too great a burden upon them. Sufficient time for prolonged deliberation is not always at hand, and not all of them are equally qualified to render the correct judgment. Objective guidance furnished by judicious legislation should be of immense assistance to them. From the standpoint of the people themselves, legislation offers a much more expedient and economic indication of where they stand before the Law.[25]

There are, moreover, many instances where the common good requires not so much that one person do this rather than that, but that the whole body of citizens act in a uniform manner. It is indifferent to peace and security what that precise manner be, but it is essential to good order that only one be elected and imposed with authority. Legislation sufficiently promulgated to the people seems the only effective means of accomplishing this purpose. All the various safety measures, especially those which involve modern means of transportation, need to be expressed in much more precise and detailed specifications than custom could offer.

The field of Law in which legislation should dominate the most is Penal Law and Penal Procedure.

> "Above all in modern times there has been evidenced an imperious demand to give legislative form to these matters, because it is precisely the penal norms which need the most certain limits, since they touch more directly upon the liberty of the citizens. Freedom of choice on the part of the judge and the wavering of public opinion are most highly dangerous here. "*Nullum crimen sine lege*" and "*Nulla poena sine lege*" are the two fundamental canons of modern penal justice."[26]

[25] Cf. Bender, *Philosophia Iuris*, pp. 209-211.

[26] Del Vecchio, *Philosophy of Law*, p. 320.

The various systems are not agreed, however, on whether the judge should be given a certain amount of discretion in determining the *degree* of punishment to be inflicted according to the circumstances of each case. Canon Law grants him considerable leeway, especially in mitigating the force of penalties.[27] Such flexibility seems to offer greater assurance that justice will be served in the majority of cases, because the judge is in a good position to estimate in what measure the fixed rules of legislation should be amended in order to apply to concrete situations. There is, in other words, a mean between complete arbitrariness and absolute inflexibilty, a mean whereby a certain amount of discretion is permitted by laws even in this dangerous field of Law.[28]

C. Jurisdiction

The term jurisdiction is taken here in its etymological sense of "*Ius dicere*," i.e., of determining what is Law in a particular controversy. The description of the judge's office is much simpler than the exercise of it. It involves a careful review of the facts and a decision rendered, for the most part, according to preexisting custom or legislation. This requires a penetrating knowledge of the Law and, most of all, a sound and mature judgment. One would hope, therefore, that appointments to these offices be independent of all political considerations. This is, unfortunately a very sore point in the practice of many States. Too much is at stake to base the selection of judges on anything other than the high qualifications they should possess.

It is usually said that jurisdiction is subordinate to custom and legislation. Although this is normally verified in closed systems of positive law, it is not entirely true in others, nor does it cover all the eventualities of a closed system. One could hardly characterize the activity of the Roman Praetor in publishing Edicts, of the Lord Chancellor of England in ruling according to "conscience," and of the medieval Popes in issuing decretals, as being completely subordinated to the other two sources of positive law.

---

[27] Cf. *C.I.C.* cc. 2223,2224.

[28] Cf. Roberti, *De Delictis et Poenis*, Vol. I, Pars II (Romae: Libraria Pontificii Instituti Utriusque Iuris, 1938), nn. 236-237.

As a matter of fact, many of the decisions of these agents of judicial power have been incorporated into the positive systems as such. In closed systems themselves, as it will be noted in the last chapter, there is place for a prudent use of equity by the judge whereby, in supplying for a lacuna in the law, he gives a positive norm of action in a particular case.

One cannot stress sufficiently the important role which jurisdiction plays in the evolution and understanding of custom and legislation. In regard to custom the judge brings to the fore the unconscious motive which lies at the heart of it. He actually detaches or abstracts the principle of Law from its living context in order to apply it to similar cases. In so doing he clarifies and develops the meaning of the custom.

> "The judicial activity, therefore, leads, first of all, to the explicit formulation of the norms which were latent or implicit in the logic of the social system actually in force. It leads also, by a natural and almost insensible transition, to the integration of such norms by means of others which are suggested, in coherence therewith, by the development and complication of the social relationships, *rebus ipsis dictantibus usu exigente et humanis necessitatibus.*" [29]

It seems that even systems which make great use of precedents do so only as a means of establishing principles of Law already in effect. The English judge is bound by a precedent only inasmuch as, by way of analogy, he finds that the principle on which the recalled decision is based applies to the case at hand. Over and above all particular precedents, he must decide in favor of the cardinal principles of the Common Law. But where even these do not suffice "and no specific decisions apply, he has recourse to natural justice, reason, morality and social utility." [30]

In this instance, it is clear that jurisdiction is no longer subordinate to custom or legislation. On the whole, however, it would be inaccurate to refer to the system of precedents as "judge-made

[29] Del Vecchio, *Philosophy of Law,* p. 309.

[30] Allen, *Law in the Making,* pp. 192-193. This seems to have been the case at the Nüremberg trials.

Law." Even where the judge can find no specific authority to guide him, he does not find himself in exactly the same position as the lawmaker. His technical training helps him to render a decision which is consistent with the general principles of his system. He does not look to the future, but acts as an interpreter of the past and present.

> ". . . but in the process of interpretation he inevitably and fundamentally affects the development of the law. He 'makes' law only in a secondary or derivative sense; but the formative effect of his interpretation on all the most essential principles of law is of the highest and most lasting importance." [31]

From what was said concerning the superiority of legislation, one may be tempted to think that in systems where judges must look to it for principles of Law, their task becomes quite simple.[32] While it is true that statutes offer easy access to the Law, they do not always dispense from a diligent study of its meaning. Laws, even such as are made by highly trained codifiers, do not always present themselves to the judge with sufficient clarity to warrant mechanical application. He, too, is faced with the problem of interpretation, with the decided advantage, however, that he may have easier recourse to authoritative clarifications. Usually his own interpretations do not impose themselves outside the orbit of the particular case decided, but they may mark the inception of a custom, which is usually considered as the best interpreter of law.[33] It seems, consequently, that even Code systems have a high regard for precedent.

SECTION 4.
TECHNIQUE OF POSITIVE LAW

Positive law represents a serious attempt on the part of man to adapt the "datum" (natural, historical, rational and ideal) to the

---

[31] Allen, *op. cit.*, p. 193.

[32] This seems, strangely enough, to be the opinion of Bender, *Philosophia Iuris*, p. 210.

[33] Perhaps this is the fundamental reason behind the high regard which the decisions of the Roman Rota enjoy throughout the Catholic Church as interpretations of Canon Law.

changing conditions of social life. Its formal sources or expressions have been studied in the preceding section. There now remains the task of examining the technique which underlies these expressions of positive law. Juridical technique may be defined as the body of constructions or operations, largely artificial, which man adds to the original "datum," in order to achieve justice amidst the complexities of society.[34] The writer hopes to give, in these few pages, only a few illustrations, mostly taken from Canon Law wherewith he is more familiar, which may incite the reader to investigate this intriguing question in competent authors such as the oft-cited Gény.[35] His main interest, moreover, is to evaluate in some measure the results one can expect from this technique in the administration of justice.

The fundamental procedure forming the basis of all positive law is that of abstraction and classification. It is a pattern which follows the structure of the human mind, something which man cannot change. In the process of abstraction, however, a whole section of life is lost, i.e., the individual circumstances in which an action takes place. All laws are general to a certain extent, some more so than others. In an effort to do justice to all, the legislator will endeavor to break down the generality of his laws into more specific particularizations. No matter how much he tries, he cannot cope with all the possible situations. In a final attempt to settle an individual problem, recourse is had to the judge who is closer to the facts. The rules of evidence and procedure offer him numerous and various devices by which he can most often ascertain the truth and apply the law with reasonable certainty that he is doing justice to the parties concerned. There will always remain cases, rare but still unfortunate, where the judge, himself bound by these abstract rules, is forced to render a decision which is, in fact, unsatisfactory.

This is, in summary, the picture of the technique of positive law, with its achievements and its failures. The latter are inherent in the nature of man's intellect. Whatever men do, they must be

[34] Gény, *Science et technique en droit privé positif*. I, n.33, pp. 96-97; III, n.183, p. 23; IV, n.273, p. 14.

[35] *Op. cit.*, especially Vol. III.

content with acting as men, and not as God. They cannot administer divine justice because they cannot read into the minds and hearts of men to sort out the motives of actions which have social overtones. They must put up with the rigidity of generalizations, and trust to imperfect intuition of concrete reality for as many corrective measures as possible. This is precisely the task of the jurist-lawyer or judge.[36] The following examples should illustrate some of these technical devices.

Canon 16 of the Code of Canon Law states the very general principle that ignorance of a law or of a personal fact is not presumed, and that it offers no excuse for the violation of invalidating laws.[37] Such a law would be the impediment of consanguinity between those persons who are related to each other within the third degree inclusively.[38] Even if such persons should marry in good faith, i.e., unaware of the law or of their blood relationship, their marriage would still be invalid (provided no dispensation was obtained beforehand). Granted that the laws in question which render this marriage invalid are necessary for the common good, is there no mitigation of the rigidness of these rules for well-intentioned people? The lawmaker does provide for some remedy with the concept of a "putative" marriage applying to these particular cases.[39] This may have far-reaching consequences for the settlement of cases involving children. Children born of a putative marriage enjoy before the law the same status of legitimacy as children born of a valid marriage.[40] From very general and somewhat harsh laws, the legislator proceeds to much more equitable particularizations.

There remains the task of the judge to apply these prescriptions to concrete cases. Let us suppose that he has to rule on an inheritance settlement, and that according to the will of the testator only legitimate children are included in the succession. He cannot accept without question the assertion of the parents that they were

[36] Cf. Renard, *La valeur de la loi* (Paris: Recueil Sirey, 1928), pp. 29 sqq.; *Le Droit, la Justice et la Volonté*, pp. 140-142.

[37] Cf. c. 11.

[38] Cf. cc. 1076, 96.

[39] C. 1015, § 4.

[40] C. 1114.

ignorant of their relationship (this is a personal fact usually of the presumption of law against such ignorance. A presumption, known among families) or of the diriment impediment, because a special technical device, is a probable conjecture concerning an uncertainty.[41] It is based on what usually occurs, and is therefore reasonable. Because there is question here of a presumption of Law, the decision will have to favor the party for whom the presumption stands, unless it is disproved by contrary evidence.[42] In this case, the burden of proof lies with the children born of the supposedly putative marriage. Upon them will fall the obligation of providing qualified witnesses[43] who can adduce arguments sufficient to overthrow the presumption. In this particular case, they may be able to show that in consequence of definite circumstances of place it was morally impossible or highly improbable that the parents involved were aware of the fact of the impediment. The contesting parties may have contrary evidence to offer. Their witnesses may give testimony which contradicts that of the first witnesses. An experienced judge, examining the witnesses separately,[44] may be able, by adroit questioning,[45] to ferret out the truth and even discover perjury on the part of some. Whenever it is necessary, he may organize a confrontation of the contradicting witnesses.[46] Finally, in his evaluation of the testimony submitted, he receives the assistance of time-honored norms relating to the integrity of the witnesses and the quality of their knowledge.[47] All these rules being applied, let it be supposed that the judge reaches the decision, one of moral certitude,[48] that the inheritance is to be denied the children of the allegedly putative marriage, because they have not sufficiently proved the good faith

[41] C. 1825.

[42] C. 1827. Since this is a "*praesumptio iuris*" only, and not a "*praesumptio iuris et de iure*," it admits of direct proof against it: cf. cc. 1825, §2, 1826.

[43] Cf. cc. 1754-1767.

[44] C. 1772, §1.

[45] Cc. 1773-1781.

[46] C. 1772, §§2,3.

[47] Cc. 1789-1791.

[48] C. 1869.

of their parents in contracting marriage. The chances are that, if the judge has painstakingly sifted the evidence and intelligently applied the rules of procedure, his decision was the correct one and in fact the true one. Actually, the truth may not have been reached. An appeal to a higher court is available,[49] but there is no guarantee that the decision will be reversed, especially if the evidence is the same. In other words, in spite of the refined norms of positive law, justice may not be served in this particular case. One comes to the realization that human justice, no matter how perfect, cannot measure up to the justice of God.

For another example of rigid classification, one may look to the status of minors in Church Law. Minors are those who have not yet reached the age of 21.[50] This is, admittedly, a somewhat arbitrary age, but a definite one must be adopted to protect the youth from their immaturity.[51] In the exercise of their Rights, they generally remain subject to the power of their parents or guardians.[52] Thus a minor retains the domicile of his parents.[53] Does this mean that a married minor, who is responsible enough to raise and support a family, cannot enjoy a proper domicile of his own? The law makes no special provision for this case, but noted canonists, repeating the customary interpretation of the pre-Code discipline, maintain that he can, on the basis that the strict classification under which he falls does not do justice to his particular situation, since he is no longer subject to his parents.[54] In many instances, the legislator himself relaxes the rigidity of this classification. Thus minors who have reached the age of puberty do have the proper Right to choose their own Church

---

[49] Cc. 1879-1891.

[50] C. 88, §1.

[51] That this is the purpose of the classification is clear from a reading of the provisions of cc. 1456; 1648, §1; 1655, §2; 1687, §1; 2204; 2218, §2; 2230.

[52] C. 89.

[53] C. 93, §1.

[54] Cf. Michiels, *Principia Generalia de Personis in Ecclesia, Commentarius Libri II Codicis Juris Canonici, Canones Praeliminares* (2.ed., penitus retractata et notabiliter aucta, Parisiis, Tornaci, Romae: Desclée, 1955), pp. 174-175.

and cemetery of burial.[55] They may act without the consent of their parents or guardians in trials involving spiritual matters.[56] Although they are exhorted not to contemplate marriage without parental consent, their union would nevertheless be valid (if they fulfill the age requirements),[57] and even licit, provided the ordinary had been previously consulted.[58]

Another technique of adaptation frequently used in Canon Law is that of dispensation. This device provides for a relaxation of a law whose observance, although generally promoting the common good, would be too demanding in a particular situation and might even derogate from the common good.[59] Perhaps the fundamental reason for the wider use of dispensations in the Church than in civil society lies in the essentially spiritual purpose of the Church. Reasonable adaptations to individual needs and circumstances seem all the more warranted when the end pursued is the ultimate end of man. To take only one example, one might consider the case of spouses who discover, after many years of conjugal life, the actual invalidity of their marriage, consequent upon some diriment impediment. Let us suppose that the latter is of ecclesiastical law, and therefore admits of dispensation. Is it not reasonable to expect that the legislator will readily grant the dispensation in order to permit this couple to continue their marital relationship and adequately care for their children?

The examples offered in this section suffice, it is hoped, to illustrate the variety of devices employed in the technical elaboration of positive law. It is a tribute to man that he has used his intellectual powers to such a high degree as to find so many ingenious methods or "trucs" to implement justice and the Natural Law. The thoughtful jurist cannot fail, at the same time, to admit very humbly that complete justice can never be achieved at this level.

---

[55] C. 1224, 1°.

[56] C. 1648, §3.

[57] C. 1067, §1.

[58] C. 1034.

[59] The general norms on dispensations are given in cc. 80-86.

Article II: The Nature of Positive Law

Under this heading the writer purports to study the essence of positive law, i.e., the psychological and moral factors which contribute to its making and also to its "obligatoriness" for subjects. For purposes of clarity, this article will deal directly only with legislation, the most explicit form of positive law, but the observations made here should apply also, *mutatis mutandis*, to custom and jurisdiction.

SECTION 1.
REASON AND WILL

No place is given here to the doctrine whereby every manifestation of the legislator's will, no matter how contrary to right reason, should be considered as a valid expression of positive law. Such a doctrine is merely an application of the theory that might makes Right, a theory already sufficiently discussed and emphatically rejected as unsound. It directly contradicts the doctrine of the Natural Law established in the previous chapter. A truly human act—and the enactment of a law ought to be that—requires a rational ordination to a rational and legitimate end. Only thus does it distinguish itself from the instinctive behavior of animals or the haphazard conduct of the mentally deranged.

In the discussion regarding the human faculties engaged in lawmaking, there is no question of effecting a choice between reason and will. Nor should one separate these two mental powers so completely as to imagine two subjects of human activity: the intellect indicating the path to follow, and the will supplying the moving force in the direction indicated. If it is necessary to distinguish the dual function of the intellect and will in the elaboration of a law, it must be remembered that there is only one subject of operation: it is man who thinks and who wills, in the unity of his intellectual substance. His activity involves two different aspects, the one illuminating and the other dynamic, represented by the intellect and the will respectively. These faculties do not alternate as distinct subjects of operation. The legislator combines their specific activity, thus issuing a rational command.[60]

[60] Cf. Sertillanges, *La philosophie des lois*, p. 15.

With these observations in mind, one is prepared to enter the age-long dispute, especially active among scholastic philosophers and theologians, concerning the essential constitution of a law. Is a law formally, principally and fundamentally an act of reason or an act of will? The writer believes that the controversy on this point, as it originated and as it persists today, resolves itself into a matter of emphasis. No one, at least, can accuse the master of either school, whether St. Thomas or Suarez, of excluding the contribution of one faculty when stressing that of the other. St. Thomas characterizes a law as an act of reason saturated with the force of the will.[61] Suarez, on the other hand, claims that a law is an act of the will impregnated with the righteousness of reason.[62] It seems, as Suarez himself states, that only the wording differs, and not the essential thought.[63] It would hardly be correct, therefore, to blame the latter for the excesses of the later "voluntarists," who forgot the important role of the intellect in the enactment of laws.

On the other hand, precisely because of the serious consequences inherent in over-emphasizing the role of the will, sometimes to the point of excluding the role of reason, a definite stand on the primary element of laws cannot be considered as a futile subtlety. The writer thinks that this is the rational element. The function of a law is to furnish rules of action. An action is well regulated when it is apt to procure what is expected of it, and that can only be obtained under certain conditions determined

---

[61] Cf. *Summa Theologiae*, IaIIae,q.90,a.1,c. & ad 3um. In the "*Sed contra*" of this article, the author states that a law is a command ("*imperium*"), and obviously refers to q.17,a.1, where he asserts that a command is essentially an act of reason because of the direction it implies.

[62] ". . . spectando ad rem ipsam, melius intelligi, et facilius defendi, legem mentalem (ut sic dicam) in ipso legislatore esse actum voluntatis iustae et rectae, quo superior vult inferiorem obligare ad hoc, vel illud faciendum. . . ."—*Tractatus de Legibus ac Deo Legislatore* (cura & studio Raphaelis Caccavo, Neapoli, 1872), L. I, c.5, n.13.

[63] ". . . quaestio fere tota erit de modo loquendi."—*Ibid.*, n.1. For a comparison between St. Thomas and Suarez on the essence of law, see Farrell, *The Natural Moral Law According to Saint Thomas and Suarez*, pp. 54-55.

by the law. There is question, then, of acute discrimination, which can be ascribed to reason alone.[64]

The following objection immediately suggests itself to this rather simple reasoning: How, according to such a definition, does a law differ from mere counsel or advice? One would have to answer that, without the contribution of the volitive element, it does not. Then, pursues the objection, why not term the law an impulsion of the will accompanied with rational indications of the directions to be followed? The only answer which can be given, but a very significant one, or so it seems to the writer, is that the directive or intellectual element is the specifically human element. It seems reasonable to consider as the formal element of a law applying to men that which appeals to his truly human characteristics. The will, as such, is without light. It lends itself to caprice, to the rule of passions, to ambition and any other inordinate desire.[65] As an impelling force, it does not differ from the instinctive appetite of animals. A law should, then, be viewed fundamentally as an intellectual expression of man's conduct. This is true of law as it emanates from the legislator and as it is executed by subjects.

A rather simple analogy will probably help to illustrate the preceding observations. What is it that distinguishes the operation of a policeman directing traffic from that of a stable-boy leading a horse to its individual stall? The motorist and the animal are both impelled by the motions of the policeman and the stable-boy respectively. The horse, on the one hand, reacts to a physical stimulus or the sensible reminiscence of the same: it is only an animal. The law officer's signs and indications, on the other hand, have an intellectual content: they are human and, as such, direct human beings. Physical impulsion may be necessary at times to enforce his directives upon those who do not heed them, in the same manner as it is used to enforce laws. But that already presupposes that the intellectual stimulus has been given.

The only point gained so far is that a law, as it exists in the mind of the legislator and as it is proposed to subjects, is primarily

---

[64] Sertillanges, *La philosophie des lois,* pp. 14-15.

[65] Sertillanges, *op. cit.,* p. 15.

an intellectual expression of what is to be done. This does not imply that a subject must find a rational justification in his own mind concerning the utility or validity of each command imposed upon him. This matter properly belongs to the "obligatoriness" of a law, and will be treated under that section.[66]

When it is said, furthermore, that the law as it exists in the mind of the legislator is primarily an intellectual expression of what is to be done, this does not mean that the legislator's will did not play an important part, and sometimes even a most decisive one, in its formulation. Very few of the dictates of positive law result from the lawmaker's will mutely acquiescing to absolutely convincing arguments logically deduced by reason alone.[67] Most often, because of the equally plausible and rational means of attaining a desired end, the will and the entire affectivity of the legislator will be the deciding factor.[68] For that reason, jurists rightly insist on the preponderance of the will in the artificial constructions of positive law, in the choice of the juridical techniques apt to implement justice in the best way possible.[69] Presumptions of law could serve as an example: the judge is commanded by the legislator to conclude in a prescribed way. The will, in most cases, certainly has a great influence over the practical

---

[66] See *below*, p. 138.

[67] "Le législateur ou le juriste ne peut accorder à la Justice tout ce qu'elle réclame: à cause des résistances de la réaction sociale: à cause de la double préoccupation coercitive et conservatrice qui domine sa mission. La Justice, les réalités, les difficultés de la contrainte, le souci de stabilisation: on n'accorde pas tous ces facteurs sans les ébrécher. Il y a de l'arbitraire dans le jugement qui sort de cette confrontation; et voilà une nouvelle porte ouverte à la volonté dans le travail de l'intelligence adonnée à l'élaboration du droit positif."—Renard, *Le Droit, La Justice et la Volonté*, p. 289.

[68] "Enfin, il ne faut pas oublier que nos diverses facultés—intelligence, volonté—sont les attributs d'une même et unique nature—qu'elles sont solidaires comme les membres d'un même organisme,—que leurs activités peuvent non seulement s'enchevêtrer, mais dans une certaine mesure se suppléer—comme le toucher supplée à la vue chez les aveugles,—et que par exemple la volonté et surtout l'affectivité pèsent d'un poids redoutable sur l'appréciation des motifs, dans la phase intellectuelle de la délibération."—Renard, *La valeur de la loi*, pp. 99-100.

[69] Cf. Gény, *Science et technique en droit privé positif*, III, 20-21.

judgment which deliberates as to what means would be more suitable to the task at hand. And it is this judgment, heavily laden with affectivity, which unlatches the act of free choice. But the law is still in its preparatory stage: its existence and texture have been decided, but it does not exist as yet. A final step is required, i.e., the actual command of the legislator by which he orients the action of his subjects, a command whose specifically human characteristic is its intelligibility.[70]

It may be objected that such a conclusion, valid from the standpoint of the philosopher, does not serve the best interests of the jurist whose chief purpose, that of assuring public security, is more surely achieved by paying attention to the decisions of the legislator than by analyzing the rational operations which prompted them.[71] Actually this objection does not disprove the foregoing conclusion. It simply justifies the primary rule of the interpretation of laws, according to which one must look first to the proper significance of the words in the text and context of a law to gather its meaning. As the adage says: "*Quod legislator voluit, ipse expressit.*" Only when the text itself lacks clarity may the interpreter search the mind of the legislator.[72] But the words of the law are signs which convey to subjects the intelligible content of the legislator's command.

SECTION 2.
COMMON GOOD AND HUMAN LIBERTY

If laws are to be reasonable, it is evident that they must serve the common good of all citizens. This section purports to study the philosophical conception of the common good and the possibility of its actual realization. The correct notion of the common good, to which so many references have been made during the course of this work, holds the key to the solution of the perennial conflicts between the so-called sovereignty of the State and the individual liberty of men. From a purely empirical viewpoint, it

[70] Cf. Lottin, "La définition classique de la loi," *Revue néo-scolastique de philosophie*, XXVII (1925), 266.

[71] Cf. Renard, *La valeur de la loi*, p. 86.

[72] Cf., v.g., *C.I.C.*, c. 18.

is generally admitted that the State has a Right to expect the service and obedience of its citizens. Anybody who openly and publicly questioned or contradicted this Right would generally be shunned by most, if not all, people. One finds, on the other hand, the same unanimity of conviction in upholding the inviolability of many individual Rights. The citizenry is adamant in claiming, for instance, the free and unhampered possession of private property. History shows that there were always proud men who refused to bow before despotism, and rebellious men who had only contempt for any social authority. At the same time, it reveals the attempts of rulers who justified their repression of both groups on the basis that they were furthering the common good. Between man and the State, there is bound to be a clash of personalities, unless there is a proper understanding of society and its common good.

In order to clear the way for more important considerations, it is important to grasp the proper meaning of the term common good. It would be incorrect to make the latter the exact equivalent of the public good, and to restrict the ambit of positive law to the promotion of public commodities and services. The common good includes the public good, but also goes beyond it. In other words, the common good of society, far from being opposed to the good of individual citizens, is directly connected with it and somehow dependent upon it. To show this is precisely the object of the present section.

A. Person and Society

Perhaps the foundation of many social aberrations lies in a misconception of society as a whole. The writer has already noted that society cannot be completely assimilated to the biological organism of the human body.[73] In the body, the parts or members have no other purpose than to serve the good of the whole. The hand will instinctively sacrifice itself to save the body, because as a being it is entirely subordinated to the good of the body. This subordination of the part to the whole is valid as a principle only when the two terms belong to the same genus, i.e., when the

[73] Cf. *above*, pp. 63-64.

part has no other subsistence than as the part of a whole. The principle does not, therefore, rigorously and infallibly apply to the relation of man to society, because, as a person, man subsists as an independent whole ordained ultimately to an immortal end which transcends society as such. This does not contradict the obvious fact of man's dependence on society. It merely qualifies it as being non-servile.[74]

Man is, indeed, a complex being. According to one aspect of his being, the purely personal aspect, he transcends society. According to the other aspect, the one resulting from his individuality, he is a part of society and inferior to it. [74a] One should, however, guard against making this distinction a separation.

> "However evident it may seem, in order to avoid misunderstandings and nonsense, we must emphasize that they (individuality and personality) are not two separate things. There is not in me one reality, called my individual, and another reality, called my person. One and the same reality is, in a certain sense an individual, and, in another sense, a person. Our whole being is an individual by reason of that in us which derives from matter, and a person by reason of that in us which derives from spirit. Similarly, the whole of a painting is a physico-chemical mixture by reason of the colouring stuff of which it is made, and the whole of it is a work of beauty by reason of the painter's art.[75]

As the same author, Maritain, says, it is the whole being of man, the human person, which is engaged in society and subordinated to it, but not by virtue of all that this person is or has. Thus a person depends heavily upon society in the process of acquiring knowledge. This condition results from the deficiencies attached to his material individuality. In this respect, man is a part of society and as such may be required by society to serve in its

---

[74] ". . . homo non ordinatur ad communitatem politicam secundum se totum et secundum omnia sua. . . ."—St. Thomas, *Summa Theologiae,* IaIIae,q.21,a.4,ad 3um.

[74a] Cf. *above,* p. 17, p. 63, note 60 a.

[75] Maritain, *The Person and the Common Good,* pp. 30-31.

general program of education. The realm of knowledge itself, on the other hand, abstracting from its manner of acquisition, is a purely personal field, one over which society has no control, because it belongs to the order of absolute goods and transcends the political community.[76] There is a whole universe of being, interior to the soul of man, which lies outside the jurisdiction of the State. It includes, besides the order of truth, the secrets of the heart, the internal freedom of action, the body of moral laws, and the individual standards of conscience. This entire realm is in itself superior to the State, and the latter can check only the external manifestations of it which are destructive of the common good.[77]

Many conclusions follow from this analysis of the human person and of the nature of society or the State. The first and most obvious is that the good of a society composed of persons cannot be understood except in relation to these persons: hence the term *common* good. Because men are not simply parts but also and eminently wholes, the good of society which they procure through their concerted activity must redound unto them as persons. The common good is not exclusively proper to society as a distinct moral person or entity: it is redistributed to the persons as "the good human life of the multitude."[78]

> "It is immediately clear that social improvement is only a means of getting at the individuals. We write new laws and abrogate old ones not to build a magnificent structure of law for its own sake nor to fashion a beautiful legal dress solely for the adornment of the state. Law is a means whose only rightful function is the service of human needs. And human needs have but one locus: the person."[79]

Society is, nevertheless, a unity distinct from its individual members. It has a political aim which does not and should not

---

[76] *Ibid.*, pp. 51-52.

[77] Cf. Maritain, *The Rights of Man and Natural Law*, pp. 42-44.

[78] Maritain, *The Person and the Common Good*, p. 36.

[79] Kreilkamp, *The Metaphysical Foundations of Thomistic Jurisprudence*, p. 26.

coincide with the interests of scattered individuals or privileged classes whose selfish ambitions may be alien to the good of the community at large. The conditions of public security, peace and prosperity over which the State watches do not automatically ensue from the striving of citizens toward their proper development and perfection. Very often the claims of some do conflict with the claims of others, and the authoritative organs of the State must step in and rule in the direction of the common good. Thus society can demand the active and intelligent collaboration of all its citizens in the furtherance of a common cause not always consistent with the egoistic standards of certain individuals. It rightly commands certain sacrifices of particular interests when the common good demands it.

To say that the State has the Right to enlist the services and sacrifices of its individual citizens because of its own proper end is just another way of restating the problem of individuality and personality in man. It is because of his individuality or individualistic tendencies that man grasps things to himself, sometimes forgetting the common good. The realm of truth and love, characteristic of the person as such, is essentially one of communication of perfection. Maritain states admirably:

> "The person as such is a whole, an open and generous whole. In truth, if human society were a society of *pure persons*, the good of society and the good of each person would be one and the same good."[80]

It is obvious that men are not mere or pure persons: they are by no means perfect. But the dignity attached to their personality redounds to their whole being. Even the material elements which enter into the composition of man share in this distinction. Man's body cannot be put on the same level as the body of any other animal, because it is the body of a person.

Applying this to the relation between man and the State, one concludes that no part of man can be used simply as a cog in the machinery of the State. No faculty of his is so inferior as to warrant its sacrifice in a manner inconsistent with the dignity of

[80] *The Person and the Common Good,* p. 42 (italics are the author's).

his nature. The aims of society are worthy of consideration only if their realization is possible through humanly dignified means. The immediate successes or achievements contingent upon the use of inhuman and therefore dishonest means lose all value in the eternal light of the dignity of the human person. One sees, therefore, the importance of these theoretical considerations in the constructions of positive law. A system which would pay little or no attention to them would defeat the purpose for which it is devised. If in its numerous and varied determinations it does not attempt, inasmuch as possible, to safeguard and serve the highest interests of man, it loses the force normally granted to it by the Natural Law.

The natural Rights of man find their full explanation in this doctrine of the person and the common good. The inalienability of these Rights, founded on the immutable nature of man, must be understood in the light of this doctrine. No Right is ever so inalienable that it knows no boundaries, not even the boundaries of the common good. To claim otherwise would be to leave out the social aspect of man's nature. There are some Rights, like the Rights to life and to happiness, whose possession cannot be restricted in any way, for this restriction itself would jeopardize the true common good of society. Their exercise, however, is sometimes subject to limitation, as in the case of the criminal who has abdicated from the order of reason. Similarly, the Right to education is limited by the practical possibilities which the particular society has to offer. In these and other cases, the possession of the Right is never questioned or limited by the common good, but only the exercise of it. It is the common good, in fact, which demands the inviolability of these Rights.

There are other Rights which are inalienable also, but only substantially, in the sense that the common good would be harmed considerably if certain restrictions could not be placed upon their very possession. Thus men do not possess freedom of speech in such an unlimited manner that they are free in any and all circumstances to express even the most pernicious errors, regardless of the effect these might have on the lives of uninformed citizens or upon the State.[81] This last problem leads to the following sub-section regarding the relation between authority and human liberty.

B. Authority And Human Liberty[82]

In order to conciliate the seemingly opposite notions of social authority and human liberty, it is necessary to dispel a few popular misconceptions of the true nature of liberty. The first consists in identifying liberty with a lack of determination.

> ". . . happy life is conceived as a continual refusal to make decisive choices, an endless succession of experiments in which the person never engages himself fully, so as to preserve and ceaselessly increase the treasury of his possibilities. Refusing to be determinately anything, trying everything without letting ourselves (to) be steadily determined in any way, we should achieve an ability to become everything, and this ability which has the taste of the infinite, is understood to be the supreme liberty."[83]

This form of indifference is a sign of poverty, what psychologists would call irresolution, rather than an assertion of the dignity of the human person. Such a state of doubt or indecision brings out the imperfect side of human freedom: it certainly cannot compare with the deliberate action of a free man exercising his mastery as a rational being over the inordinate drives of his passions. A passive indetermination of a faculty which prevents man from engaging his whole personality in the pursuit of perfection cannot possibly be the truly great asset of human freedom. It is unthinkable that men should have died for such an imperfect possession.[84]

---

[81] Cf. Maritain, *Man and the State*, pp. 97-103. The writer is deeply indebted to the works of Maritain for most of the considerations appearing under this sub-section concerning the person and the common good.

[82] In these few pages, the writer owes much to the excellent article of Yves Simon, "Liberty and Authority," *Proceedings of the American Catholic Philosophical Association, The Problem of Liberty* (Washington, D.C.: The Catholic University of America), XVI (1940), 86-114.

[83] Simon, "art. cit.," pp. 94-95.

[84] A person who prizes this side of freedom would probably be classified by Kierkegaard (1813-1855) as living in the Don Juan stage of existence. "It includes the attitude of those who hate fixed lines and definite

The true and perfect form of indifference inherent in liberty consists in an active domination of the will over the various possibilities of action that are presented to man by his reason. This indifference is present in its highest degree when man has reached such a state of determination (perfection) that he can exercise complete domination over the attractive aspect of any action. It should be noted that if man were in possession of his ultimate end, thus achieving the greatest degree of determination, he would enjoy the utmost freedom in regard to things not necessarily related to it. He would completely dominate his life and his actions. The indifference which was present in his will would be transferred to the objects attracting his will. In other words, he would be so completely the master of himself because of having achieved his destiny, that no other apparent good could impose itself upon him.

Such perfection is not possible here on this earth, but great strides can be made toward it. The only end unmistakably given by nature is the abstract form of the ultimate end, the good as such. There is no choice possible in regard to the end as such, because it fulfills the notion of good which prompts man's every action. Freedom lies only in the choice of means. The imperfection of human freedom attaches to the possibility of electing certain courses of action which are really inconsistent with the attainment of the end in question. Any determination, therefore, which would remove this possibility by offering a more penetrating grasp of the true end and of the order to this end (*ordo finis*) would liberate freedom from its heaviest burden. It is clear, then, that freedom is not extolled by the ability to choose evil, another popular misconception.

The first application of these principles to society is quite clear. If social life has as its foremost purpose to leave man in a state

---

contours, who wish to taste all experiences, to put on all characters, who strive after a 'false infinity'. The aesthetic man refuses to recognize and to choose himself, to commit himself; anything which binds him down and gives shape and definiteness to his life, such as morality and religion, he rejects."—Copleston, *Contemporary Philosophy, Studies of Logical Positivism and Existentialism* (Westminster, Md.: The Newman Press, 1956), p. 151.

of passive indifference and indecision, it is doing him an injustice under the illusion of favoring his liberty.

> "The crudest form of the illusion is the 'primitive liberty' which the disciple of Rousseau thought he had found again in the wilderness of the new world. Wandering in the forest, he took pleasure in zigzagging along just to assert his freedom from the straight path uniformly traced by human societies . . . Conversely, liberty is promoted by any social background and environment that gives the individual more firmness, more cool-headedness, more self-control, more clear-sightedness, a more lucid insight into his own aspirations and the end he has to pursue." [85]

The purpose of positive law is to provide sufficient determination in citizens to enable them to collaborate actively and intelligently in the pursuit of their common perfection. In persons who are incapable of governing themselves, as children and feeble-minded persons, the function of authority will be entirely substitutional. For that matter, the great majority of men will suffer considerable hardships if they do not receive authoritative guidance throughout their lives. Even in the supposition that men were perfectly capable, by reason of their intelligence and virtue, to conduct their own lives, the concerted actions tending to the realization of the common good would still require the exercise of authority. Very few courses of action present themselves with such evidence and necessity that would lead to the unanimity of conduct which, in certain instances, is so necessary to the common good.[86]

Regulations imposed upon men for the sake of the common good do not take away the interior spontaneity of action which is one of the characteristics of personality. Rid of the possibility of making wrong choices (at least to a great extent), the citizen asserts his increased dominating power over all the possibilities open to him by agreeing spontaneously with the precepts of the law, by making the law interior to his own will. No man is so

[85] Simon, "art. cit.," pp. 94-95.
[86] Simon, *ibid.*, pp. 101-103.

perfect that he can always and from the beginning so dominate the circumstances of his life that he infallibly chooses the course which really leads to personal achievement and development. Social authority is ever present to liberate him from his infirmities and help him to attain true freedom.

This does not imply that the holders of governmental authority are infallible. There are instances where their government openly conflicts with justice, with the dignity of the person and human liberty. This situation will be studied in the next chapter.[87] Chances are, however, that the positive law in force, being the result of a careful and wise adaptation of all the data of human experience to present-day situations, offers the best possible course of conduct to the subjects over which it rules.

It is important to note also that State authority cannot, without defeating the purpose already outlined for it, substitute itself entirely or arbitrarily for private initiative. It is sometimes necessary, for the reasons given above, for the State to control those enterprises which more directly affect the public good. But if the State were to intervene in all matters of social concern, it would deprive the people of the opportunity to exercise their freedom spontaneously, and would reduce them to mere puppets in the hands of the State. The pluralistic principle should be sedulously applied, according to which every enterprise which can be effectively conducted through the personal efforts of individuals should not be subject to undue and excessive control on the part of the State. Even if the results are not as immediately successful as they might be in a State-controlled affair, society will have gained in the long run from the personal development of its citizens. And only thus will the common good, the good of persons, be truly achieved.

> "Human life as a whole . . . is orientated towards the fulfillment of the needs and demands of personal existence. As in the individual, so in society, the fullest measure of personal living is the goal to which all efforts to organize, direct, govern and control the instrumentalities of human progress should be directed. It is only through intensely *personal* living

---

[87] Cf. *below*, pp. 154-162.

> that men can realize the full potentialities of personality and become, what by nature and grace they are destined to become, viz. complete human persons. But, persons are beings who own themselves and are masters of their actions. That is but another way of saying that they are free."[88]

With these principles in mind, one is in a better position to judge within what limits the Right of freedom of expression may be exercised. It is certain, first of all, that not every thought, simply because it evolved in the mind of a free person, is worthy of being spread about society. For the sake of the common good, the State has the Right to censor and restrict the expression of ideas which are subversive, i.e., which undermine governmental authority and suggest that the government itself be overthrown by whatever means necessary. This is especially true if the circumstances in which this takes place present a serious threat to public security. Actually this is another instance of authoritative guidance which, far from destroying freedom of expression, insures its most perfect realization. Man's knowledge progresses slowly: in infancy, his first steps toward truth are under the direction of selected masters. In the area of political truths, which by no means belong, for the most part, to the order of clear and easily accessible evidence, most men remain beginners throughout their lives, and this sometimes in regard to issues vital to social peace. They can therefore benefit by the wise and sober direction of authority. One may also consider "censorship" useful, if applied with discretion, in other fields less political, such as the sensationalism of the press in crime reports.

If, in view of the common good, the State has the Right to curb freedom of expression to a certain degree, and even with recourse to authoritative censorship when absolutely necessary, the exercise of this function must never be such as to completely silence the voice of the citizens. As a matter of fact, the State does better in providing, through the media of mass communication, a vast pro-

[88] Phelan, "Person and Liberty," *Proceedings of the American Catholic Philosophical Association, The Problem of Liberty* (Wash., D.C.: The Catholic University of America), XVI (1940), 65-66.

gram of civic education than in making wide use of physical restrictions and censorship. Thought is, in fact, irrepressive, and it is preferable that the State direct it in the proper channels by encouraging the initiative of certain groups of men devoted to a study of political and moral problems. If the people are thus properly instructed in the vital issues of social life, they themselves will be capable of checking in a much more effective and personal manner the immoral activities of social perverts or heretics.

C. Practical Realization of the Common Good

The writer has often remarked that the practical application of principles is much more difficult than their rational exposition. To speak *in abstracto* of what the common good should entail in order to meet the requirements of human personality which it is called upon to serve does not automatically solve all the practical problems involved in this realization. As it was noted in the preceding article of this chapter, there are many instances where measures demanded by the "theoretical" common good would seriously conflict with the "practical" common good. The actual moral standards of a people or of a civilization determine to a great extent just how perfect a realization of the theoretical common good can be achieved. In other words, although the principles of justice and human dignity (correlatives of the common good) are objective and immutable, the means of implementing them will vary according to the moral tone of the people for whom they are applied. Thus the concrete goods offered under the notion of the common good will also vary from age to age, from civilization to civilization.[89]

This realistic view, which seems the only sensible one, should not lead to a fatalistic attitude, in the sense that society is doomed to remain within the limits of its present realization of the common good. Innovations always disturb the social peace to a certain degree, but not all of them should be suppressed on this account. If they are demanded by the people's awakening to a higher understanding of their dignity as human beings, they deserve serious

[89] Cf. Maritain, *Man and the State*, pp. 61-64.

consideration on the part of the State, and careful integration into the pattern of social life. The growing recognition given today to the Rights of the worker is a good case in point. Not all of the desired reforms have been made as yet: measures of this sort cannot be achieved overnight. It is nevertheless quite certain that no modern society can be said to procure the common good (in its practical and possible realization) if it does not endeavor to enforce the Rights of the working class.

SECTION 3.
"OBLIGATORINESS" OF POSITIVE LAW

The writer intends to show in this section that citizens are morally bound in conscience to obey all just laws imposed authoritatively by the governing powers under which they live. He feels, furthermore, that to speak of the necessity of obedience to these dictates without first studying, if only briefly, the principles of legitimacy of governmental authority would leave a serious gap in his exposition. Another section will deal with the problem of promulgation, a necessary pre-requisite to the "obligatoriness" of laws.

A. Legitimate Government

It is outside the scope of this general work to even outline the innumerous doctrines on this point, with their infinitesimal "nuances" or shades of meaning.[90] The most fundamental principle is that which absolutely requires some form of government in any determined society. It is one that is as surely founded on the Natural Law as the sociability of man upon which it rests. If you take away the necessity of authority, you take away the possibility of achieving the common good, and thus the very purpose for which men join in society.[91] One should note immediately that governmental authority traces its origin in human nature and not in the will of the people. Certain modifications will be adduced later in clarification of this statement, but it is important to assert

[90] For this, see Leclercq, *Leçons de droit naturel*, Vol. II: L'Etat ou *la politique*, pp. 135-172. It is in this author that the writer has found the most satisfying doctrine on the legitimacy of a government.

[91] See *above*, pp. 127-129. See also Leclercq, *ibid.*, pp. 125-134.

from the beginning that authority is grounded in nature, and ultimately has its source in the Author of nature. Government is too basic and absolute a social need to place its foundation in the often fickle and sometimes divided will of the people.

The second principle, one which plays as important a part as the first one because it is an explicitation of it, states that the powers of government are limited by the mission which the latter is called upon to achieve, i.e., the procurement of the common good. No human government may be invested with absolute powers. If it is clearly shown that the actual rulers do not serve the true interests (common good) of the people, they lose their Right to govern, no matter how much popularity they may enjoy among citizens. This assertion may seem radical at first glance; it certainly must be understood in the light of the "practical" common good explained in the previous section.[92] Only a grave, permanent and general abuse of power causes a government to lose its legitimate authority.[93]

According to a third principle which enters into the picture, no man has the power of and by himself to exact the obedience of his fellowmen. This is but an expression of the fundamental equality of men. How is it that one man or one group of men acquire this power of domination? The clearest solution would result from an explicit manifestation of the mind of God, the source of all authority. Experience teaches that such is not the usual occurrence. As a matter of fact, some men do emerge from the multitude with unmistakable qualities of leadership. But the number of men endowed with such aptitudes may very well surpass the number needed to form a government, and it would still be necessary to make some selection. The normal manner of achieving this lies in the common consent of the people. This does not mean that the power to rule comes from the common will of the people, but that in the normal course of events the actual holders of this power will be chosen by them, for want of any other manifestation of the will of God.

---

[92] Cf. *above*, p. 130-131.

[93] The conditions of legitimate resistance to such a government will be studied in the next chapter. See *below*, pp. 158-162.

To affirm as a general principle, then, that authority derives from God but always through the will of the people does not seem to be correct, at least not in the manner in which it is usually understood. This takes care of the greatest number of cases, but does not provide for emergency cases wherein the common good demands a ruling authority and the population is too unsettled to provide a definite one. In this respect, it seems that the government which certain dictators or military leaders establish by force in times of civil strife or popular rebellion against the acting regime cannot automatically be called illegitimate, provided that it restores peace and security and thus ensures the realization of the common good.[93a] In these cases of necessity, the people have a duty to obey these leaders. It seems that the primary principle in this matter is that of the common good, and not the supremacy of the people's will. There are circumstances, although perhaps less frequent today, especially in democratic systems, where only one man or a small group of men is capable of procuring this common good.[94] It is the latter, in these instances, which gives them the Right to take over the reins of government and to require the dutiful obedience of subjects. And again, it is the very same common good which demands that, when circumstances indicate that the time for emergency measures has passed, the voice of the people be given its normal function. In other words, when there is a possibility of choice (within the common good) it belongs to the people. The manifestation of this choice need not always be explicit, as in democratic elections. Tacit ratification of a traditional procedure, as in a government by monarchic succession, would be sufficient. Consequently, if in normal circumstances a

---

[93a] It is supposed here that the conditions required for legitimate resistance are fulfilled. Cf. *below*, pp.

[94] According to Leclercq, one example of this took place in the case of General de Gaulle at the liberation of France in 1944. The former quotes Léon Blum (1872-1950) in this matter: "Si le pouvoir que le général de Gaulle exerce est légitime, ce n'est pas parce qu'il a été le premier résistant de France ou le chef des résistants en France, c'est parce que, par un concours de circonstances, il s'est trouvé le seul homme à pouvoir rassembler autour de son nom la totalité des forces de la France libérée. C'est là son titre.'"—*Leçons de droit naturel*, II, p. 174, n.1.

dictator imposes himself by force on the people, his authority is considered illegitimate. There are, of course, doubtful cases which cannot be settled at the level of abstraction now being used here: each individual case has to be studied on its own merits. For the sake of the common good which requires an abiding form of government, the presumption stands in favor of the actually ruling and rightfully established authority.

B. Promulgation of Laws

Whatever be the mode of promulgation in the various systems of positive law, all agree on its necessity. The very nature of a law, its general definition as a rule and measure of acts, as the guiding principle leading to the common good, and as the command of the ruler, necessitate its diffusion among the public. It seems to the writer that the age-long dispute among scholastics as to whether promulgation is of the essence of a law or only a necessary pre-requisite of its application to subjects is a matter of terminology. To be sure, the ways and means adopted by a government to make the law known to its subjects are not essential elements of the law itself. They are only signs which manifest its content. It seems quite clear to the writer, however, that it is futile to speak of a command to subjects which does not have the notion of publicity attached to its very essence. Because the problem is entirely theoretical, there seems to be no reason to pursue it further.[95]

A more serious and practical difficulty lies in the general assumption that, once a law has been promulgated and the time (if any) has elapsed between its promulgation and the date set for its effectiveness, all the people know of it. This position abstracts from the question of moral guilt when a person violates a law unknown to him. The fact remains that he may be prosecuted and condemned for his transgression in the courts of positive law. The official method of promulgating laws today is normally through

---

[95] For ampler details and subtle distinctions, see the exposition (which the writer adopts) of Michiels, *Normae Generales Juris Canonici,* I, 180-192. See also, Lohmuller, *The Promulgation of Law,* The Catholic University of America Canon Law Studies, n. 241 (Washington, D. C.: The Catholic University of America Press, 1947), pp. 28 ff.

technical journals. This makes it theoretically possible for all to gain a knowledge of the law.

In practice, however, the matter is not so simple. Although new laws are generally publicized in the press, there remains the fact that many people, particularly those of the lower class of education, do not read the newspapers, or at least not the sections which deal with legislation. The matter is further complicated because only the technically trained are capable of grasping the full impact of laws as they first emanate from authority. Customary observance of them will be the decisive answer in the long run, but that takes time. Instruction in the schools and a wide and judicious use of all the media of mass communication will prove useful in the meantime, but never wholly adequate.

Despite all these practical difficulties (another point evidencing the inability of positive law to promote absolute justice), the common good demands that the general presumption of the knowledge of a law be upheld. Actually promulgation creates a *praesumptio iuris et de iure* of knowledge, except perhaps in regard to criminal law, where positive law often makes special provisions. The necessity of certainty in juridical relationships precludes, as a general rule, basing a juridical ordinance "upon so precarious a footing as would be the knowledge of the law which would have to be shown each time for each single citizen."[96] Various systems of positive law do, however, offer some remedy for the situation explained above, by recognizing, in certain instances, the existence of excusing causes. Canon Law, for example, states as a general rule that a fact concerning others which is not notorious does not come under the wide presumption of knowledge.[97] While this does not treat directly of the ignorance of a law, it certainly will affect the application of a law in view of this extraneous fact whose knowledge is not presumed. It is mainly in the question of penalties that Church Law makes judicious distinctions: between culpable and non-culpable ignorance, negligent or malicious

[96] Del Vecchio, *Philosophy of Law*, p. 312. The author's brief but penetrating treatment of the problem is the one expressed here by the writer.

[97] *C.I.C.*, c. 16, §2.

ignorance, ignorance of a law having an automatic penal sanction and of one requiring a judicial infliction of a penalty, ignorance of a law whose wording implies full deliberation and consent and of one which does not contain such a wording.[98] With these and other similar restrictions, it is certainly justifiable to argue in favor of the general presumption of knowledge of the law.

C. Moral Obligation of Positive Laws

Many modern jurists contend that civil laws have no moral purpose contained in them. They simply strive to contain the excesses of citizens within boundaries set up to satisfy the exigencies of public peace, prosperity and security. This doctrine obviously stems from a false conception of the juridical order, separating it entirely from the moral order: a conception which the writer has studied above and rejected.[99] Whatever be the private intention of the legislator, if he enacts laws compatible with the common good, with the natural precepts of justice properly applied to social life, he is inevitably engaged in the noble process of rendering citizens virtuous. The common good is, in fact, a part of the total good of man, a means (already good in itself because it is an intermediate end) to the ultimate perfection he is ordained to achieve. Since it is redistributed to the individual members of society, the common good cannot help but enrich the whole man in his moral development. The very fact that citizens willingly submit to legitimate authority already marks a notable step in this direction, because it denotes some rational appreciation of the immeasurable service rendered to them by civil laws.

With these considerations in mind, one readily understands that the moral obligation of positive laws results from the necessity of each citizen to strive toward the common good, the latter being itself founded on the Natural Law, and ultimately on the Eternal Law of God. When a person deliberately and willingly obeys just civil laws, he does not yield to arbitrary force but to the necessary pursuit, rationally perceived, of his ultimate end. Such dignified submission to laws already implies, especially in its constancy, a

[98] Cf. *ibid.*, cc. 2199, 2202, 2229.

[99] Cf. pp. 38-39.

high degree of virtue. Inasmuch as this cannot be expected of all citizens, a juridical or social constraint is called upon to assist and supplement the interior command of reason or of the properly so-called moral obligation. However necessary this assistance appears, especially for beginners (and men always remain beginners to some extent), it cannot secure the common good as effectively as a deep sense of moral obligation. If the expression may be permitted, constraint alone may procure the common good of automatons or animals: it cannot succeed in achieving the common good of human beings, persons whose dignity requires an intelligent and willful collaboration in the purpose they pursue. If constraint or the fear of coercion does not lead to this form of action, it falls short of its mark. In a society where it is alone to provide respect for authority, there is felt a gradual degeneration which tends to social disorder. The police power can cope with occasional but not community-wide violations. And even if it could, it would hardly benefit a society fit for humans.

The true authority of the legislator lies, in this doctrine of moral obligation, in its accord with justice. Only under this supposition does he have the Right to the obedience of his subjects.[100] It is significant to note that this doctrine does not, according to the present writer, allow for any exception in the necessary obedience to just laws. The theory of "purely penal" laws, elaborated by scholastic philosophers and theologians, may have brought out the fact that the violation of some laws is of minor gravity. The opinion according to which certain laws do not bind to the accomplishment or omission of the act but only to the penalty prescribed for the certified violation of these laws does not, or so the writer feels, deserve recognition. If a law is just, if it is commanded in virtue of the common good, it requires obedience, regardless of how closely the law is connected with its ends, as, v.g., in traffic regulations. It is difficult, furthermore, to see how any punishment could be justly inflicted upon the violators of these "purely penal" laws.[101]

---

[100] The possibility and conditions of resistance to unjust laws are not envisaged here; they will be studied in the next chapter. Cf. pp. 154-162.

[101] For a thorough exposition and refutation of the theory of "purely

The common good demands a further precision, in the sense that dictates of the lawmaker be strengthened with a favorable presumption, the presumption that they do conform to justice and tend toward the good of the citizens. Experience teaches that, in general, this is a reasonable presumption with respect to both the government and its subjects. Laws are, as a rule, the product of mature deliberation and a well directed desire to improve the social life of the citizens. It is to be expected also that legislative bodies are well trained in the techniques of good government. Considerations such as these offer a sound basis for subjects to presume that the laws imposed upon them are worthy of their whole-hearted obedience.

It is not even necessary nor is it possible for most men that they clearly perceive the good sense and social utility of these laws. Some understanding of their purpose, supplied by public authority, is desirable in order to enlist a more conscious and active collaboration on their part. Even without any such understanding, however, submission to authority is not unreasonable. It is necessary, furthermore, that the primary psychological motive for it lie in the favorable if unverified presumption of justice granted to all laws emanating from authority.

No social life could survive if each member were allowed to verify and justify in his own mind the reasonableness of laws before yielding to them. Of course, a presumption is only a conjecture: however legitimate in its generality, it is sometimes overruled by fact. In this event, man finds himself in the presence of a real conflict between positive law and Natural Law, which forms part of the subject-matter treated in the next and last chapter of this work.

---

penal" laws, see Renard, *La théorie des* LEGES MERE POENALES (Paris: Recueil Sirey, 1929). The author reproduces, in his conclusion, the opinion of Bishop d'Hulst (1841-1896) according to which many violations of what others consider to be "purely penal" laws would be disregarded because of the extreme slightness of matter. The writer would be prepared to go along with a discreet exposition of this view: "De minimis non curat praetor," "The better is often the enemy of the good."—Cf. *ibid.*, pp. 75-76.

Chapter IV: CONFLICTS BETWEEN POSITIVE LAW AND NATURAL LAW

Introduction:

The writer has often alluded, especially in the previous chapter, to the possibility of conflicts between the enactments of positive legislation and the dictates of the Natural Law.[1] Most of these result from an imperfect, albeit sincere, attempt on the part of positive law to approximate the Natural Law. The circumstances with which human lawmakers must contend in the elaboration of positive systems of law preclude an absolute realization of natural justice. Since in many instances nothing better can be achieved, it would be incorrect to look upon these results as truly and directly conflicting with the Natural Law. The first article of this chapter will consider at some length one example of this kind, namely the law of prescription. Later in the same article, special attention will be focused on the role of equity in adjusting positive legislation to the Natural Law. The second article will study the juridical and moral problems raised by laws which directly conflict with the Natural Law.

Article I: Apparent or Indirect Conflicts

SECTION 1.

THE EXAMPLE OF PRESCRIPTION

In its broadest sense, the term prescription denotes a means of acquiring a Right, of repelling an action, or of extinguishing an obligation, given by law to one who for a definite period of time has been in possession of a Right or who in fact has been free from satisfying an obligation.[2] To this general notion correspond

---

[1] See *above*, pp. 98-101, 130-131.

[2] Cf. Vermeersch, *Quaestiones de Justitia ad usum hodiernum scholastice disputatae* (Brugis: Beyaert; Romae-Ratisbonae: F. Pustet; Lutetiae Parisiorum: P. Lethielleux, 1901), p. 335 (hereafter cited *Quaestiones de Justitia*).

three distinct yet related entities of American and English Law: adverse possession, prescription and limitation of actions.[3] It is not the writer's intention to give a detailed account of the law of prescription or of the conditions of its application. His only purpose is to resolve the apparent conflict it sometimes establishes with the Natural Law. For the sake of clarity, the writer will use the term prescription mainly to signify a means whereby one acquires title to something which, before the prescribed time required by law has elapsed, is the rightful property of someone else.

It is quite clear that ownership acquired by prescription does not directly derive from the Natural Law. There is no strict connection between acquisition of title to property and the actual possession of it for, say, ten or twenty years. Nor is there any natural relation between the lack of actual possession, for a certain period, of an object rightfully owned and the ensuing loss of title. On the contrary, it would seem at first glance that by dispossessing a party of his title through prescription one sins directly against the natural principle of rendering to each person his due.

Joannes Andreae, a noted medieval canonist (1270-1348), seemed to say that the common opinion of the jurists of his time held prescription to be contrary to the Natural Law, on the basis that it allows the enrichment of one at the expense and injury of another.[4] The eminent commentator believed, on the contrary, that this opinion derived from a misunderstanding of the role of positive law in relation to the Natural Law. According to him, positive law adds certain specifications to the "rectitude" of Natural Law. It determines, for instance, the degree of punishment to be inflicted for various crimes. It also clarifies the data of Natural Law by applying them to concrete situations. Thus it accepts the natural principle that no one should be enriched from

---

[3] For a proper definition of these three entities, see Martin, *Adverse Possession, Prescription and Limitation of Actions, The Canonical "Praescriptio," A Commentary on Canon* 1508, The Catholic University of America Canon Law Studies, n.202 (Wash., D.C.: The Catholic University of America Press, 1944), pp. 3-4 (hereafter cited *Adverse Possession*).

[4] *In Titulum de Regulis Iuris Novella Commentaria* (Venetiis, 1581), In Regula n.2: *"Possessor malae fidei ullo tempore non praescribit,"* fol. 58 va. (hereafter cited *De Regulis Iuris*).

damage and injury done to another. At the same time, it points out (something which the Natural Law cannot do) certain cases wherein it is possible for one to gain from damage done to another without violating this person's Rights. In this way, it explains the meaning of a particular dictate of the Natural Law.[5]

This, contends Joannes Andreae, is precisely the role of positive law in the case of prescription. It is evident that the person whose property yields under prescription to another party suffers a real damage. And yet there is no injustice because, so stated the author, he thereby receives due punishment for having neglected to attend to his property.[6] The argument, as advanced so far, is not absolutely convincing. The law recognizes the juridical value of prescription even in cases of non-culpable neglect. With this objection probably in mind, the canonist goes on to give the decisive reason in favor of prescription: the common and public good of the community. Without prescription, the rightful ownership of property remains forever uncertain, and thus gives rise to innumerable conflicts and disputes which trouble common peace and security.[7] In other words, by allowing prescription, positive law clarifies the rule that no person should enrich himself at the expense of another by exempting those cases wherein this is demanded by the common good. Thus a particular precept of the

---

[5] ". . . ius legale (positive law) quandoque assumit rectitudinem iuris naturalis, et eam specificat declarando per quosdam eventus. Verbi gratia, assumit a iure naturali quod rectum est neminem cum alterius detrimento et iniuria fieri locupletiorem. Non tamen potest haberi a dicto iure, utrum sit possibilis aliquis eventus, vel casus, in quo quis possit locupletari cum alterius detrimento, et sine eius iniuria; et ideo specificat postea, et declarat intellectum dictae regulae in quibusdam casibus."—*Ibid.*, fol. 58 va,b.

[6] *Ibid.*, fol. 58vb.

[7] ". . . si usucapio et praescriptio tolluntur, receditur ab illa regula iuris naturae, quae dicit quod bonum publicum et commune est praeferendum cuicumque bono speciali et proprio; in remotione autem praescriptionis et usucapionis fit totum contrarium, praeeligitur bonum proprium illius, qui negligit repetere rem suam, et dat materiam litium, et rixarum, et per consequens praemittitur bonum commune, quod consistit in pacifico communitatis convictu; nam data materia litium et rixarum per remotionem praescriptionis et usucapionis convictus communitatis pacificus perturbatur. . . ."—*Loc. cit.*

Natural Law is to be understood in the light of all the others, and applied in such a way as not to contradict a higher principle: in this case, the particular good is subordinated to the higher common good of society.[8]

Thus spoke an author of the Middle Ages in favor of prescription. The arguments deployed by more modern authors may have been somewhat polished but they remain basically the same.[9] They all show quite convincingly that in its general notion prescription offers no true or direct conflict with the Natural Law.

There remains to be studied the important question regarding the necessity of good faith in the person acquiring title by prescription. Good faith may be defined as a prudent judgment according to which a person believes that the thing he possesses is rightfully his. Philosophers and theologians have, on the whole, concurred in requiring good faith, even for the entire period of the running of prescription.[10] Any other conception seems, at least in the case of acquisitive prescription, to open the door to theft and general dishonesty. As one author puts it, even relatively good men would be willing to endure moral guilt for a few years if after a certain

---

[8] *Loc. cit.* See also *above*, pp. 65-68, 89.

[9] Cf., v.g., Schmalzgrueber, *Jus Ecclesiasticum Universum brevi methodo ad discentium utilitatem explicatum seu lucubrationes canonicae in quinque libros decretalium Gregorii IX Pontificis Maximi* (Romae, 1843-1845), Lib. III, tit. xxvi, nn.4,8-12 (hereafter cited *Jus Ecclesiasticum*); Reiffenstuel, *Jus Canonicum Universum complectens Tractatum de Regulis Iuris* (Parisiis, 1866-1870), Lib. II, tit. xxvi, nn. 19-23 (hereafter cited *Jus Canonicum Universum*); Vermeersch, *Quaestiones de Justitia*, pp. 341-344; Cronin, *The Science of Ethics*, II, 147-148.

[10] The IV General Council of the Lateran (1215) settled the matter for the conscience of Catholics: "Quoniam 'omne . . . quod non est ex fide, peccatum est' [Rom.14,23], synodali iudicio diffinimus, ut nulla valeat absque bona fide praescriptio tam canonica quam civilis, cum generaliter sit omni constitutioni atque consuetudini derogandum, quae absque mortali peccato non potest observari. Unde oportet, ut, qui praescribit, in nulla temporis parte rei habeat conscientiam alienae."—Denzinger, *Enchiridion Symbolorum, Definitionum et Declarationum de Rebus Fidei et Morum*, denuo compositum a Clemente Bannwart et curis iteratis editum a Ioanne Baptista Umberg (ed. 24-25., Barcelona: Editorial Herder, 1948), n. 439. For the correct understanding of this decree, see Vermeersch, *op. cit.*, pp. 339-341.

period of time they could achieve rightful and honest possession.[11] In such a hypothesis, prescription would certainly be contrary to the Natural Law, inasmuch as it encouraged widespread dishonesty among citizens, a state or condition certainly harmful to the common good, to public peace and security.

As a matter of fact, positive laws on prescription generally require good faith.[12] This was not always the case. Roman Law required it, as a rule, only at the beginning of possession. A person could thus possess in bad faith for a great length of time and then acquire rightful ownership.[13] Even in modern societies, there are instances of positive laws which, especially in long-term prescription, consider only the question of initial good faith.[14]

One's first reaction to laws such as these would be to condemn them as absolutely unjust and invalid because of their direct opposition to the Natural Law. Schmalzgrueber (1663-1735), for one, taught that such laws were rightly abrogated by Canon Law.[15] No civil constitution, so he contended, may lend its authority to sinful actions and even favor them with the protection of law.[16] This categorically strict view certainly is in concord with the "theoretical" common good of society. There is no doubt that, if positive law were dealing with an abstract conception of the common good, it would be forced to deny any validity to prescription in bad faith. As a matter of fact, however, the governmental authority of societies must be content with an imperfect realization of that common good, which has earlier been called the "practical" common good.[17]

---

[11] Cronin, *The Science of Ethics,* II, 149.

[12] For American Law, v.g., see Martin, *Adverse Possession,* pp. 32-33, 36-38, 48-53.

[13] Cf. Buckland, *A Manual of Roman Private Law,* pp. 126-129.

[14] See articles 2262 and 2269 of the French Civil Code, cited by Laprat, "Prescription," *Dictionnaire de Théologie Catholique,* ed. A. Vacant, E. Mangenot & E. Amann (Paris: Letouzey et Ané, 1903—), Tom. XIII (1936), col. 124-125.

[15] ". . . leges illae civiles admittentes praescriptionem cum mala fide, per jus canonicum merito abrogatae sunt, cujus constitutio, cum agatur de periculo animae, etiam in foro civili est observanda."—*Op. cit.,* Lib. III, tit. xxvi, n. 57.

[16] *Ibid.,* n.60.

[17] Cf. *above,* pp. 130-131.

If at times positive law recognizes the validity of prescription, one should not, it seems, conclude that it directly puts a premium on dishonesty. Actually, in its realistic approach to the common good of society, it may feel that it is better, given the present moral standards of the people and the circumstances in which they live, to look to the benefits derived from the settlement of disputes by prescription than to insist on the freedom of guilt in the person who puts prescription to use.[18] One should consider also that prescription is originally a procedural device (limitation of actions), which looks not so much to the acquisition of title as to the consequence of silence on the part of the other party, i.e., the barring of an action. This attitude is consistent with the doctrine of the scholastics which admits that human law cannot enjoin the exercise of all the virtues or forbid the practice of all the vices, but that it must sometimes permit or tolerate certain evils for the sake of safeguarding a higher order of good.[19] One can conclude that in general the positive laws on prescription, even those which do not require good faith, are not necessarily in direct opposition to the Natural Law.

SECTION 2.
THE PROBLEM OF EQUITY

One of the usual characteristics of a law, although not an essential one, is its generality. Most laws are the product of abstraction, i.e., they abstract from the singularities of life and are intended to apply to a whole series of cases of the same type. This abstraction from individual circumstances, without which no uniform rule of conduct could be formed, looks to the normal course of

---

[18] ". . . ius civile cum intendat pro ultimo fine conservare civilem societatem, cui fini maxime deservit negligentia, punitio, et litium determinatio, idcirco magis debet intendere ad hoc, ut negligentes puniat, et finem litibus imponat, quam ut iniquitatem praescribentis corrigat, vel removeat; nam magis ad ipsum spectat illius duplicis finis aequitas prosequenda, quam ipsius praescribentis iniquitas corrigenda."—Joannes Andreae, *De Regulis Iuris,* fol. 59va. The same author pointed out that it belongs rather to Church Law, whose purpose is mainly the spiritual welfare of souls, to guard against bad faith in prescription. This would explain why Canon Law always requires good faith. Cf. *C.I.C.,* c. 1508.

[19] Cf. St. Thomas, *Summa Theologiae,* IaIIae, q. 96,a.2.

events, to what usually takes place in society. It is a process determined by the exigencies and limits of the human mind. The rigidity of the rules thus elaborated has an over-all beneficial effect in the government of the people. It affords stability and precision to juridical life, and offers a sure guide to follow in civil and commercial affairs. No person, for instance, would dare enter into a contract fraught with risks if at the same time he did not feel the assurance of an abiding and fixed system of laws protecting him.[20]

The formulation of abstract rules is, however, only the first step in the attempt of positive law to implement justice. There remains the all-important task of applying these norms to concrete cases. From the world of rigid and absolute concepts in which laws are made there has to be a descent into the world of living and changing reality where no two cases are completely alike. Sometimes the transition is relatively easy, i.e., when the circumstances which surround the case in question are quite the same as those probably envisaged by the lawmaker. In these instances, although individuals might suffer certain inconveniences and even hardships from the observance or application of the law, the benefits accruing to society in the name of public security must be given primary consideration.

> ". . . the law and lawyers often have to bear hard words. Too frequently the layman, loud in his condemnation of 'flagrant injustice,' will not attempt to look beyond the particular to the general, which it is exactly the business of the lawyer to do, and which must be done by somebody, if society is not to fall to pieces. Too often the law is denounced in the same manner as the whole science of surgery might be denounced

---

[20] "Arbitraire pour arbitraire, celui des formes abstraites préconstituées est habituellement le moins redoutable. Les formes juridiques éprouvées par l'expérience, enracinées dans la coutume ou authentiquées par le législateur, impriment à la vie juridique une stabilité, une sureté, une fermeté, une précision, qui sont le premier besoin des affaires civiles, commerciales ou administratives. Leur rigidité, leur quasi-automatisme, permettent de prévoir et de calculer; grâce à elles, on sait où l'on va et l'on ose se risquer. . . ."—Renard, *Le Droit, la Justice et la Volonté,* pp. 55-56.

> because a single patient dies under the knife. It must be admitted—and it is a source of genuine regret to every lawyer who respects his profession—that the law, like surgery, 'loses' a certain number of patients; but its instrument is not, as some seem to think, that of the butcher, but of the healer."[21]

There are, on the other hand, circumstances which so completely affect and change the nature of a situation that the rigorous application of the normal rule for cases of its kind would offend man's sense of natural justice. There is felt the need of a moderating or discretionary influence to adapt, modify or even correct laws in order that they may justly apply to singular cases. This, in general, is the role of equity.

The notion of equity is not a new one. The Greeks were perhaps the first to express it in philosophical terms. Plato (427-347 B.C.) pointed out in his *Statesman*:

> "The difference of men and actions, and the endless irregular movements of human things, do not admit of any universal and simple rule . . . A perfectly simple principle can never be applied to a state of things which is the reverse of simple."[22]

Aristotle (384-322 B.C.)offered his solution for the problem when he stated:

> ". . . the equitable is just, but not the legally just, but a correction of legal justice. The reason is that all law is universal, but about some things it is not possible to make a universal statement which shall be correct. In those cases, then, in which it is necessary to speak universally, but not possible to do so correctly, the law takes the usual case, though it is not ignorant of the possibility of error. And it is none the less correct; for the error is not in the law but in the nature of the thing, since the matter of practical affairs is of this kind from the start. When the law speaks universally, then, and a case arises on it which is not covered by

---

[21] Allen, *Law in the Making*, p. 198.

[22] *The Dialogues of Plato*, trans. by B. Jowett (2 vols., 13th printing, New York: Random House), II, 294.

> the universal statement, then it is right, where the legislator fails us and has erred by over-simplicity, to correct the omission—to say what the legislator himself would have said had he been present, and would have put into his law if he had known . . . And this is the nature of the equitable, a correction of law where it is defective owing to its universality." [23]

In this conception, then, equity is viewed as a superior form of justice, a method of adaptation whereby the strict legal rule of positive law is corrected in a certain manner to fit the realities of juridical life. It is an attempt to make sure that positive legislation achieve the purpose of natural justice which it is meant to serve by relinquishing some of its artificial stiffness or rigidity.

It is not the writer's purpose to discuss in great detail the influence of this philosophical view in the systems of positive law that were established thereafter. The fact stands out that all systems have admitted the need of tempering, to some extent, the harshness resulting from the generality of laws. As a matter of fact, the beginnings of most systems are marked by the recognition of extensive powers of this kind accorded to certain judiciary organs. The extreme formalism usually associated with the primitive stages of legislation in a given system requires the counterbalancing influence of some such moderating authority. One recalls, for instance, the all-important activity of the Roman Praetor granting actions and exceptions to actions which were not provided for by the laws in effect at that time. These modifications, founded for the most part on the Praetor's appreciation of the naturally just, and published in the form of Edicts, became known as the *ius honorarium* or magisterial law. Although it was not legislation in the true sense of the word, it had the happy effect of satisfying the just claims of individuals in certain situations not covered by the *ius civile*. It thus brought remedies to the sometimes excessive rigor of existing legislation.[24]

One finds the same remedial and corrective activity at work in

---

[23] *Nicomachean Ethics*, Bk.V,Ch.10, from *The Basic Works of Aristotle*, ed. by McKeon (12th printing, New York: Random House), 1137b, 10-30.

[24] See Jolowicz, *Historical Introduction to the Study of Roman Law* (2. ed., Cambridge: The University Press, 1952), pp. 95-99.

the English system of law. Although English equity has practically become today a jurisdiction quite distinct from the Common Law, it began in much the same way as the *ius honorarium* of the Romans. This time the discretionary power was in the hands of the King's Council, and later on of the Lord Chancellor alone. Their guiding principles were, not so much the letter of the Common Law, but rather that form of natural righteousness, taught by philosophers and theologians of that time, which considers all the particular circumstances of the deed, tempering justice with mercy.[25]

It would be incorrect to assume that equity was the product only of those who possessed extraordinary powers of discretion, such as the Roman Praetor or the English Chancellor. Under the Roman classical jurists, it took on the task of attempting to achieve perfect equality for all under the law. The various expressions of *aequitas, aequum et bonum, utilitas, humanitas, benignitas, ratio naturalis* and *bona fides* appear almost everywhere in Roman Law, and contrive to establish a benign and benevolent interpretation of the strict rules of law. This form of equity was counselled by Ulpian (170-228) when he wrote: "*In summa, aequitatem quoque ante oculos habere debet iudex.*"[26] A similar admonition to judges was incorporated into Justinian's codification in the words of Constantine and Licinius: "Placuit in omnibus rebus praecipuam esse iustitiae aequitatisque quam stricti iuris rationem."[27]

The Christian influence, represented by the teachings of the Fathers of the Church and the medieval canonists and theologians, was very partial to the notion of equity. Although the term *aequitas* was not always used in the same context, emphasis was placed on a number of institutions such as dispensation, indulgence, mercy, humanity and pardon, which manifested the same funda-

[25] See Allen, *Law in the Making*, pp. 212-231. The author regrets that equity has become, in English Law, the prerogative of a separate jurisdiction: "We have no cause whatever to consider our methods superior to those of other nations who have kept their equity as an integral part of the law of the land, and not as the close preserve of a specialized jurisdiction which has too often made a laudable end subservient to questionable means."—*Ibid.*, p. 231.

[26] *Digesta* (13,4)4, Quod si Ephesi, § 1.

[27] *Codex* (3,1)8; (3,38)12.

mental idea, i.e., a benevolent interpretation or modification of a strict or rigorous law.[28]

The philosophical development of the notion of equity acquired a renewed impetus during the Renaissance, with a rediscovery of the *epikeia* of Aristotle and the discussion by scholastics of the doctrines of St. Thomas and Suarez on this point. Both of these authors considered *epikeia* as a correction of the law which failed in a particular case because of its universality. There was, however, a notable divergence between the two. St. Thomas felt that the correction was to be made when the law failed to such an extent that, if applied to a particular case, it would contradict the Natural Law or the exigencies of the common good. Thus it was the *power* of the legislator that was questioned here. Suarez, benefiting from the developments of the medieval canonists, adopted a much broader view. He felt that *epikeia* applied when it could be at least probably presumed that, owing to the extenuating circumstances of the case at hand, the legislator did not intend to oblige the subject to the observance of the law, although its clear words would otherwise demand compliance with it. The emphasis was, then, on the *will* of the legislator.[29] Although the preoccupation of moral theologians, following St. Thomas and Suarez, was focused on the problem of the conscience of individuals before the law, it cannot be denied that the notion of *epikeia*, as they understood it, was inspired by the broader concept of equity.[30]

---

[28] On this point see the erudite work of Lefebvre, *Les pouvoirs du juge en droit canonique, Contribution historique et doctrinale à l'étude du canon 20 sur la méthode et les sources en droit positif* (Paris: Recueil Sirey, 1938, esp. pp. 164-186; also the article by the same author: "Equité," *Dictionnaire de Droit Canonique,* ed. par A. Villien, E. Magnin, A. Amanieu, R. Naz (Paris: Letouzey et Ané, 1924—), V (1953), col. 396-399.

[29] The latter is the definition adopted by Riley, *The History, Nature and Use of EPIKEIA in Moral Theology,* The Catholic University of America Studies in Sacred Theology, 2. series, n.17 (Washington, D.C.: The Catholic University of America Press, 1948), p. 137. The author gives a detailed analysis of the doctrines of St. Thomas and Suarez at pp. 28-52 and 67-80 respectively. For the author's own explanation of the nature and use of *epikeia,* see pp. 133-195.

[30] For the dispute among authors as to the relation of *epikeia* to equity, see Riley, *op. cit.,* pp. 230-236; Lefebvre, "Epikie," *Dictionnaire de Droit*

This brief historical review suffices, it seems, to show that equity has exhibited itself in two principal forms. The first, which could be called *equity in general,* inspires a liberal and humane interpretation of the law without actual derogation from it. Sometimes this is expressly indicated in the law: it is what the medieval canonists called *aequitas scripta*; but in most cases, the legislator is presumed to be animated with benevolent rather than severe intentions. The second form of equity, referred to as *particular equity,* is "a liberal and humane modification of the law in exceptional cases not coming within the ambit of the general rule." [31] With this distinction duly understood, it will be somewhat easier to broach the delicate subject as to whether it is advisable to allow the use of equity in positive systems.

As regards *equity in general,* most jurists seem to admit that it may be applied. As a matter of fact, its legitimacy seems to be embodied in the rules of interpretation sanctioned by most systems of law. Although the judge's first position is to inspect the words of the law (*quod legislator voluit ipse expressit*) and to apply them as they read, he is not always limited to such an action. If he is convinced that the letter of the law would offend justice rather than serve it, he is allowed to investigate its spirit and thus seek a more humane and liberal, i.e., equitable, application of it. Very often, if he studies the end of the law and the expressed or presumed mind of the legislator, added to the circumstances in which the law was enacted, he will achieve a better insight into its meaning. Thus, while still applying the law, he will play an important role in realizing its purpose of justice.

Sometimes the borderline is very thin between the use of *equity in general* in the interpretation and application of a law and that of *particular equity* in the modification of it. It seems that it is the failure to recognize this fact which has lead certain jurists to deny that a judge may at times modify the law to a certain extent in order to do justice to a given case. As a matter of fact, in similar instances, his duty of rendering a decision may force

Canonique, V, col. 364-365; Michiels, *Normae Generales Juris Canonici,* I, 566-568.

[31] Allen, *Law in the Making,* p. 197.

him to create a new norm applicable to the situation at hand. This possibility has been severely attacked by many jurists in their desire to protect society against the arbitrariness of the "government of judges." It would certainly be preferable that there be no *lacunae* in positive law, thus guarding against the dangers inherent in the use of *special equity*. It is certain, however, that the multiplication and refinement of laws can never succeed in covering all the possible circumstances in which juridical relationships evolve. In the interpretation of laws, the "*ratio legis*" and the "*mens legislatoris*" can be stretched only up to a given point, beyond which the meaning of the words used in the law changes completely, and there takes place the creation of a new norm.[32]

It may be of interest to outline briefly the solution which Canon Law has brought to the problem of equity.[33] Besides the numerous instances where the legislator either explicitly or implicitly commands the use of equity,[34] there are two general situations in which the intervention of equity is required in virtue of the theory of law adopted in the canonical system. This theory, although nowhere expressed in the Code, has been developed over the centuries by the analyses and observations of canonists reflecting on the spirit of Church legislation. Its major point asserts the equitable character of a law, in the sense that the intention of the legislator is limited by the actual exigencies of the common good of the Catholic Church. Because of the inevitably universal character of a law, it sometimes happens that the reasonableness it enjoys in its general formulation is lost in view of the particular circumstances in which its application is sought.[35]

The two situations in which a law fails to retain its ordination

---

[32] For a thorough discussion of the problem of *lacunae* in positive law, see Lefebvre, *Les pouvoirs du juge en droit canonique*, pp. 13-66.

[33] The substance of what follows is taken from Lefebvre, "Le rôle de l'équité en droit canonique," *Ephemerides Juris Canonici* (Romae: Officium Libri Catholici, 1945—), VII (1951), 137-153.

[34] Cf. idem, "art. cit.," pp. 138-144, where many canons of the Code of Canon Law are cited.

[35] See the developments of Van Hove, *De Legibus Ecclesiasticis, Commentarium Lovaniense in Codicem Iuris Canonici*, Vol. I, t.2 (Mechliniae-Romae: Dessain, 1930), pp. 90 ff.

to the common good, and therefore its reasonableness, are those which were envisaged by St. Thomas and Suarez. The first considers the possibility of a direct clash or conflict, where the observance of a purely ecclesiastical law would entail a direct violation of the Natural Law. It is presumed that the lawmaker did not or could not foresee such an occurrence. In any case, his sovereignty cannot impose itself on subjects in matters directly opposed to natural precepts of conduct. There is, in other words, a natural boundary beyond which his power does not hold.

The situation envisioned by Suarez and admitted by canonical jurisprudence is much more complex. It involves a set of circumstances, judiciously examined, which contrive to render the observance of a law (always purely ecclesiastical, and therefore positive) gravely inconvenient or practically impossible. In these instances a judge may render a prudent decision that, although the legislator retains the power to impose obedience, he is presumed not to want to do so under the extenuating circumstances.

There is no doubt that the use of equity, as outlined in these two general situations, is fraught with great dangers. It is feared that either the Rights of individual parties or the common interests of the ecclesiastical body will suffer from excessive arbitrariness on the part of the judge. Canonical tradition has always been aware of this problem, as is intimated in the constant condemnation of "*aequitas cerebrina.*" [86] While deciding, nevertheless, in favor of admitting the use of equity, it has set up a whole network of guideposts which the judge or any other person employing equity must follow.[87]

It is asserted, first of all, that the circumstances in which this form of equity (*special equity*) may be used must be extraordinary, and therefore very rare, indeed. This is particularly true in the case of a law based on the presumption of public danger, whose

[86] Cf. Reiffenstuel, *Jus Canonicum Universum,* Lib. I, tit.2, § xvi, nn. 415-417.

[87] The writer cannot examine all of these conditions in the present article. See, v.g., the observations of Riley (*op. cit.,* pp. 133-195), which, although directly concerned with *epikeia,* apply *mutatis mutandis* to equity.

gravity imposes a much stricter compliance with it.[38] In doubtful situations, the required course of action is always in favor of the observance of the law. Furthermore, all the methods of correctly interpreting and applying the law must have been previously exhausted. And in all cases the difficulty excusing from obedience must not be intrinsic to the law itself, but must derive from some exceptional cause or event. Thus, for instance, the normal hardships inherent in the law of celibacy present no valid reason for ever excusing from it.

To these and other general restrictions commonly taught by canonists and moralists, the Code of Canon Law itself adds certain other indications.

> "Si certa de re desit expressum praescriptum legis sive generalis sive particularis, norma sumenda est, nisi agatur de poenis applicandis, a legibus latis in similibus; a generalibus iuris principiis cum aequitate canonica servatis; a stylo et praxi Curiae Romanae; a communi constantique sententia doctorum." [39]

Although the Code here directly intends to offer guidance to a judge who must supply a positive norm of action in the case of a lacuna, there is no doubt that these prescriptions apply also to the negative aspect of equity, i.e., that of excuse from the observance of a given law. One could say, in brief, that the canonical system sanctions no other than that trained sense of equity, one that is familiar with the entire body of legislation, the general principles which support its structure, the longstanding practice and jurisprudence of the Roman Congregations and Tribunals, and the common and constant opinion of canonists at large. All these are practical guarantees against the excesses of an arbitrary or flighty use of equity.[40]

---

[38] "Leges latae ad praecavendum periculum generale, urgent, etiamsi in casu peculiari periculum non adsit."—*C.I.C.*, c.21.

[39] C. 20.

[40] For an excellent study of these factors, see Lefebvre, *Les pouvoirs du juge en droit canonique*, pp. 97-304. See also Michiels, *Normae Generales Juris Canonici*, I, pp. 585-637.

Article II: Legitimate Resistance to Unjust Laws

SECTION 1. PRELIMINARY CONSIDERATIONS

For those who admit no other norm of justice than that set forth by the actual ruling authority, the problem of legitimate resistance to unjust laws does not present itself at all. For that matter, a truly positivistic frame of mind precludes the rendering of any theoretical judgment regarding human values, i.e., what ought to be. The whole tenor of this dissertation militates against such a point of view. There is a difference between Right and wrong, between justice and injustice. In practice, it may not always be easy to discern it, but it is there for perspicacious and prudent men to discover.

It is necessary, at the outset of this article, to distinguish carefully between two kinds or species of unjust laws. The first comprises enactments which command the performance of decidedly immoral acts. A decree obliging all candidates to political office to renounce their religious convictions serves as a good example. Under no circumstances is it ever permissible to comply with such a law. On the basis that it is better to obey God than men, it is necessary to suffer the consequences, sometimes very harsh, rather than perform an intrinsically evil deed. This is the glorious but tragic story of martyrdom which mankind has written on many pages of its history. Unjust laws belonging to the second species are those which, although not compelling men to act immorally, nevertheless fail to respect their duly constituted Rights and justice in general. To use a clear example, a law subjecting men to strict slavery, i.e., considering them as things rather than as human beings, would come under that classification of unjust laws. Certain tax laws which are completely out of proportion either to the needs of the government or to the means of the subjects also belong to that category. Inasmuch as these laws do not dictate an evil act, one might still, under the circumstances to be outlined below, have to obey them, and precisely in virtue of Natural Law principles.

A second distinction which imposes itself here is that of passive and active resistance. Resistance is called passive if it consists simply in refusing to comply with a law while submitting to the punishments which may be inflicted as a consequence. If it is true, as it was said above, that opposition of this kind is mandatory in the face of laws which command an evil act, the same cannot necessarily be said concerning one's attitude toward otherwise unjust laws, i.e., those belonging to the second category mentioned. Citizens are said to resist actively when they deploy concerted means to obtain the reforms which they deem necessary. This form of resistance becomes legal or illegal depending upon the quality of the means used. And even if in certain circumstances violent measures are permissible it does not inevitably follow that all forms of violence will be legitimate. Except when the opposite is indicated in the context, the following discussion is concerned with illegal active resistance to unjust laws.[40a]

In all cases where there appears a contrast, more or less sharp, between natural justice and the solemn command of written law, great importance is to be attached to the attitude first adopted or, in other words, to the primary principle of solution which is accepted. Looking at the matter from the point of view of the hierarchy of values alone, it would seem that the Natural Law, which is the primordial expression of justice since it emanates from the ultimate source of justice, i.e., God, should be given the immediate preference over the sometimes arbitrary or artificial dictates of positive law. This position, while it rightfully recognizes the theoretical supremacy of the Natural Law, fails to perceive its full import. A correct understanding of natural justice, placing the necessity of order under normal circumstances at the head of all other principles of social life, demands that the fundamental attitude of citizens be directed to the acceptance of governmental authority over and above the requirements of certain individual precepts of the Natural Law (always under the supposition that the laws do not command intrinsically evil actions). To use the words of Gény, it is from a superior Natural Law that there arises the necessary hegemony of positive law.[41]

[40a] Note that in this context "illegal" is not synonymous with "illegitimate." It is opposed to "legal," i.e., that which is permitted under positive law.

[41] *Science et technique en droit privé positif*, IV, 76-77.

In this apparent paradox, one sees better than ever the intimate connection between Natural Law and positive law. The necessary order postulated by the nature of society, by the Natural Law, is that which gives the greatest strength to the dictates of the actual holders of power. Over and above the short-range reasonableness of laws, their rational ordination to particular ends, greater emphasis should be laid on the fact that they are closely-knit pieces of the plan of general order so vital to social peace and security. The first reaction of a good citizen, therefore, should always be to want to preserve this order, even in spite of the hardships or sacrifices this may cost him. If he were to assert unconditionally that he is always entitled to resist the violation of his Rights, he would manifest a gross misconception of the role of positive law in society. In other words, resistance even to unjust laws is not legitimate when it disturbs the social order in a manner disproportionate with the benefits to be derived. As Rommen says, "the continuance of any order at all, however mixed with injustice and arbitrariness, is of greater value than the utter lack of order, than total disorder."[42]

It is obvious, then, that if under certain circumstances the Right of resistance or insurrection is recognized, it will not be in virtue of the doctrine of so-called individualistic liberalism. In the view adopted here, there is no place for an insincere resignation to the fact of positive legislation, as if it were a necessary evil restricting the use of individual freedom. Nor is there room for any general sentiment of distrust toward the lawmaker which could always expect the worse from him.[43]

A true understanding of the value of positive law will, in the case of conflicts with the Natural Law, lead, first of all, to the use of all the legitimate means capable of effecting the desired reforms.

> "Justice itself imposes the obligation that one recognize and preserve, first of all, that portion of justice which must still be incorporated in the system in existence, whatever may be

[42] *The Natural Law*, p. 200.

[43] Cf. Rommen, *op. cit.*, p. 199.

its imperfections, and that, without endangering those germs and nuclei which are alive, one work over them, within the limits of the system, to bring them to greater development. Whoever knows, and every jurist knows it, what a wide margin the positive juridical formulations necessarily leave to the interpreter, and how every system, even though apparently 'closed,' has in reality its 'valves' and its natural means of renovation, of transformation and of growth, cannot fail to recognize this elementary requirement that even when faced with unjust ordinances one should have recourse first of all to these means, and should not lightly or arbitrarily destroy that which is built up with great difficulty."[44]

In some systems, perhaps more than others, the legal means for the correction of unjust legislation are more readily available. This is especially true in constitutional regimes, proper to most civilized nations: the popular elections to the legislature, the control exercised by the mass media of publicity, the division of the legislative body into two distinct Houses, the power of veto of the executive branch, all these are effective measures which reduce the number of unjust laws, or which allow for corrections of past mistakes. The rigid articles of the constitution itself, which usually express in solemn fashion the general principles of objective justice, offer a precious guarantee to one whose Rights are threatened. In the supreme courts of most States, an exception of unconstitutionality is given due consideration regardless of the social standing of the petitioner or the defendant.[45]

No system, however, is so perfect as to prevent all abuses of power. History, and not necessarily ancient history, reveals that many of the revolutions which took place were entirely justified in view of the intolerable conditions to which the people were subjected. It is also a matter of acquired experience that the reforms effected by some of these were well worth the temporary disorder caused by the rebellion. One author goes so far as to say that

[44] Del Vecchio, *Philosophy of Law*, pp. 455-456.

[45] For a fuller explanation of these and other preventive or repressive means of opposition to unjust laws, see Gény, *Science et technique en droit privé positif*, IV, 78-112.

the most decisive advances in civilization and law are the product of revolutions.[46] They are, in many instances, inspired by the ideal of a more perfect realization of law and order. It should be pointed out, also, that the constant possibility of revolutions holds tyranny in check, and secures to a great extent the maintenance of individual Rights. If the holders of governmental power could be assured of their positions by virtue of a doctrine absolutely condemning open and active resistance, they would more easily tend to despotism.[47] These considerations should not be taken as a universal approval of all revolutions. Some are pure disorders and achieve nothing but further disorder. There remains, nevertheless, the possibility of just revolutions, under certain well-defined conditions now to be examined.

SECTION 2.
GENERAL CONDITIONS FOR LEGITIMATE RESISTANCE

The injustice against which one rebels must be, first of all, of such a nature that it appears certain and self-evident to any impartial observer. If it were admitted that every movement of individual conscience were sufficient to authorize the rejection of laws along with insurrection, the very foundation of objective justice would crumble. Law and order cannot survive if the validity of each legislative enactment is made to depend on the unanimous approval of all subjects. It is worth recalling here some of the remarks made in connection with the certainty of the Natural Law.[48]

The defense of a Right only doubtfully vindicated by the Natural Law cannot serve as a legitimate reason for refusing to obey a law or for inciting to rebellion. The disturbance to social peace caused by revolutions should not hinge on intangible motives, especially since the imposition of a law by a rightfully recognized authority offers a presumably sound and certain course of action. Accordingly in cases of doubt a person should favor the accept-

---

[46] Gény, *op. cit.*, IV, 115.
[47] Gény, *op. cit.*, IV, 133-134.
[48] Cf. *above*, pp. 85-88.

ance of even seemingly unjust laws rather than trust to his own more fallible judgment.

> "It must be kept in mind that quite different motives can lead one to attack the established juridical order. It can be the purest aspiration toward a more perfect justice, and it can be the egoistic desire to subtract oneself from one's own duties . . . Too often the 'revolutionary spirit' has abused the sacred name of justice to cover impure passions and unilateral interests." [49]

In this line of thought, then, one would have to conclude that in practice a legitimate basis for active resistance would be found only in the maintenance of those individual and family Rights which are easily recognizable by all.[50] It seems, also, that resistance would not be legitimate if it were undertaken for the defense of only one individual or one family.

Another condition attached to the Right of active resistance is usually expressed in terms of its grave necessity. This restriction, as all the others discussed here, is also commanded by the superior requirements of stability, security and order, all of which spell out the great good of peace in society. No social progress is possible without the latter. Consequently the very possibility of legitimate resistance as well as the extent of it are measured according and in proportion to the benefits inherent in the desired reforms. Only a very grave injustice can justify rebellion of any kind, and if the objectives can be obtained by less violent means, such as strikes, boycotting, etc., one does not have the Right to have recourse to arms. It is easier to admit the legitimacy of resistance through lesser violence, than that which resorts to open warfare.[51]

---

[49] Del Vecchio, *Philosophy of Law*, p. 455.

[50] Gény, *op. cit.*,IV, 120. The author also points out (pp. 121-122) that resistance should come from the individuals whose Rights are attacked, and not from the agents of the State whose duty it is to judge according to the laws. While the present writer admits this as a general rule, he feels that there may be circumstances which would permit and even at times demand that certain officials of the government lead the revolutionary movement. This is especially true when the situation evidently demands a change and they are the only ones capable of promoting it. Cf. *above*, p. 133.

[51] Cf. Leclercq, *Leçons de droit naturel*, II, 186-188. As the author says, a theoretical exposition cannot offer much more precise norms of apprecia-

Even if all the preceding conditions are fulfilled, it is possible that there be no Right to active resistance. Regardless of how manifestly tyrannical a government may be, a revolt will not be justified unless it has some warranted chances of success.[51a] If the revolutionary movement is so disorderly that it cannot hope to improve on even the very imperfect order maintained by tyranny, it fails to meet the requirements for its legitimacy. This principle is sometimes borne out by the existence of counter-revolutions striving to remedy the evil effects of prior rebellions.

It would seem, however, that the principle just enounced smacks of opportunism, at least at first glance, and that it cannot be verified except *a posteriori*.[52] Who would have thought, for instance, that a miserably and poorly armed country like Spain could succeed against Napoleon, who had established a regular government there, and who was then at the height of his power? And yet it did. The revolt of Ireland in 1920 against the English nation, then dominating the world, is another example of seeming folly converted to prudent foresight by actual success. The Catholic Church has often been criticized and even accused of duplicity in this matter. Its doctors and theologians reprove the uprisings of those unfortunates who rebel without a warranted (or so it seems) chance of success. If perchance they do succeed in achieving reforms and in reestablishing order, it is quick to support the authority of the now victorious government. Actually such an attitude, although apparently opportunistic, does not deserve all the bitter condemnations it has sometimes received. It is commanded, in fact, by the necessity of emphasizing the respect for already established order. It is preferable to accept whatever order exists than to consent to futile

---

tion. This is left to the prudent and practical judgment of the people concerned.

[51a] This is true more especially from an objective standpoint. It does not imply necessarily that the rebels themselves are always morally guilty whenever they rise up against tyranny without actual chances of success. Crises of that sort do not usually allow for a clear and cool judgment, and therefore much if not all of the moral culpability is sometimes excluded. The Hungarian revolt of 1956 could serve as a good example of this.

[52] On this point, see Leclercq, *op. cit.*, II, 186-188, 198-202, whose thoughts are substantially reproduced here.

civil wars which only bring on more social confusion. On the other hand, if a revolutionary movement does succeed in imposing itself and forming a satisfactory government, that same principle of public order demands that it be accepted rather than that a prolonged strife be engaged in. In other words, the Church and the Natural Law, instead of playing favorites, consider that some government is better than no government at all. This same attitude is reflected in the general doctrine of international law (not accepted by the United States in the case of Communist China), whereby revolutionary governments must be given recognition if they have, *de facto*, been firmly established.

There remains the delicate question of deciding when a revolution has chances of success. This is a practical question and the most penetrating legal theorists are not always the best counsellors. It is not sufficient to examine coldly the material means over which the revolutionary movement has control in the conduct of its campaign. Even if these are inferior to the ones at the disposal of the ruling powers, the intense desire for reform which animates the rebels may seem sufficient to turn the tide in their favor. Only those who are cognizant of all these factors can give a prudent decision in such difficult and intricate matters.[53]

Some modern authors raise the objection that revolutions should be outlawed altogether because they are inevitably accompanied by abuses of their own. The excesses of violence prompted by the effervescence of passions seem to be the common lot of all rebellions. It should be remembered, first of all, that it is usually necessary to take very strong measures to oppose tyranny and successfully overthrow it. It is impossible and unrealistic, furthermore, to expect that in the heat of resistance all of the combatants

[53] "S'il faut se défier des passions, il faut donc se défier aussi de la pusillanimité des théoriciens. Les questions politiques ne se résolvent pas en alignant des principes; elles exigent le jugement pratique qui suppose la hardiesse, la clairvoyance des situations concrètes, l'esprit de décision et le courage de porter de lourdes responsabilités. Ces vertus se trouvent plus souvent chez les hommes d'action que chez les hommes de cabinet."—Leclercq, *op. cit.*, II, 199. The author goes on (pp. 200-202) to give the example of the last civil war in Spain, where, says he, it is doubtful if history will ever be able to tell if the revolutionary movement was legitimate.

will retain complete control over their senses and passions. If this is commonly understood in normal events, how much more should it be in the circumstances now envisaged. There is also, as in many other cases, a sharp distinction to be made between the principle and its correct application. It is incorrect to deny the validity of a principle on the basis of the possible abuses attached to its application. The best that can be done is to counsel moderation with the hope that such directions be heeded.

It seems legitimate to conclude, with Gény, that "resistance to oppression, judiciously understood, wisely contained within its specific objectives, led with tact, remains . . . the supreme palladium of justice and law." [54]

---

[54] ". . . la résistance à l'oppression, judicieusement comprise, sagement contenue en ses lignes directrices, maniée avic tact, demeure . . . le palladium suprême de la justice et du droit."—*Op. cit.*, IV, 133-134.

CONCLUSIONS

1. It seems incorrect, in philosophical parlance, to define a Right primarily as a moral faculty or power. To say that a person enjoys a Right means that there is a relation of necessity between that person and the actions or omissions of others in regard to the object of that Right.
2. Man becomes the subject of Right because he is endowed with a rational nature, and not because he is *actually* capable of eliciting normal rational acts.
3. The coercibility of a Right, i.e., the lawfulness of defending a Right, is to be carefully distinguished from the physical possibility of enforcing it. The former, but not the latter, is a necessary consequence of the enjoyment of a Right.
4. Although the citizen must normally yield the exercise of the coercibility of his Rights, he does not lose this coercibility entirely and irrevocably. He may at times, v.g., to guard against immediate unjust aggression, use physical force of his own to defend his Rights.
5. It is incorrect to advocate a complete divorce of the juridical order from the moral order. The latter, regulating the entire sphere of man's activity in regard to necessary ends, includes the good of social justice so essential to man, which is assured by the juridical order.
6. The opinion which denies any juridical value to the Natural Law leads to absurd conclusions, even to the denial of the same value to positive law, since the force of the latter is based on the former.
7. Even today the main reason why the Natural Law is rejected by many jurists lies in its association with the false doctrine of the 17th and 18th centuries, according to which the Natural Law would be a super-system of positive law regulating all actions up to the minutest details and imposing itself upon all nations alike.

8. The Natural Law can be defined as a body of rational dictates resulting from man's grasp of the necessary order implied in the relation of his faculties or appetites to their natural ends, and in the co-ordinate or subordinate relation of these ends to the integration of the whole self.
9. Man's knowledge of the Natural Law is still incomplete or imperfect. Many of its ultimate determinations are uncertain and, therefore, it is sometimes difficult to discern the exact point of demarcation between the Natural Law and positive law.
10. One should be careful not to lay undue emphasis on the immutability of the Natural Law. A precept dealing with the intrinsic ordering of a human faculty to its natural end admits of no exceptions in any sense. One, however, which protects a particular good may be limited by another of the same category, or subordinated to a principle governing a higher good.
11. It would be unreasonable to expect that positive law could meet the requirements of all the principles of the Natural Law taken separately. The circumstances of its formulation, application and enforcement allow only an imperfect approximation of the Natural Law. Therein lies a paradox whereby the Natural Law itself commands that a positive system be content with a partial realization of the common good, what the writer has called the "practical" common good.
12. The various systems of positive law give evidence, in most instances, of man's admirable ingenuity in perfecting techniques which serve to implement justice as well as possible.
13. Positive law must be reasonable, i.e., it must direct men to rational goals via rational means. While it is true that a law is primarily an act of the legislator's intellect appealing to the intellect of citizens, one must not forget the important contribution of the legislator's will in selecting one course of action among many possible courses.
14. Human liberty does not truly suffer from a wise form of direction and control exercised by a government endowed with authority. Laws imposed upon men help them achieve

a more perfect stage of freedom than would be possible if they were left entirely to their own counsel.

15. All just laws oblige in conscience. This ensues directly from the intimate connection between the juridical and moral orders, between positive law and the Natural Law.
16. Many of the conflicts between positive law and the Natural Law are unavoidable, in the sense that they result from the former's imperfect realization of the "theoretical" common good.
17. In many instances, the rigidness and consequent harshness inherent in the generality of positive law can and should be corrected by a trained and prudent sense and use of equity on the part of the judge.
18. The necessity of preserving social order requires that citizens normally comply even with unjust laws, provided that they do not command the performance of intrinsically evil acts. Only under very strict conditions is it ever legitimate to enter upon a course of open and active resistance. Within these limits, however, the possibility of resistance has a restraining effect on the ruling powers.

BIBLIOGRAPHY

SOURCES

Acta Apostolicae Sedis, Commentarium Officiale, Romae, 1909-1929; Civitate Vaticana, 1929—

Codex Iuris Canonici Pii X Pontificis Maximi iussu digestus, Benedicti Papae XV auctoritate promulgatus, Praefatione, Fontium Annotatione et Indice Analytico-Alphabetico ab Emo Petro Card. Gasparri Auctus, Romae: Typis Polyglottis Vaticanis, 1917; reimpressio, 1934.

Corpus Iuris Civilis, 3 vols., Vol. I, *Institutiones*, quas recognovit P. Krueger; *Digesta*, quae recognovit T. Mommsen et retractavit P. Krueger, ed. stereotypa 15.; Vol. II, *Codex Iustinianus*, quem recognovit et rectractavit P. Krueger, ed. stereotypa 10., Vol. III, *Novellae Constitutiones*, ed. stereotypa 5., a R. Schoell; opus Schoellii morte interceptum absolvit G. Kroll, Berolini: apud Weidmannos, 1928-1929.

REFERENCE WORKS

Allen, Carleton Kemp, *Law in the Making*, Oxford: Clarendon Press, 1927.

Aristotle, *Nicomachean Ethics*, from *The Basic Works of Aristotle*, ed. by Richard McKeon, 12. printing, New York: Random House, copyright 1941.

Bender, Ludovicus, *Philosophia Iuris*, 2. ed., Romae: Officium Libri Catholici, 1955.

Blais, Hervé, *Les tendances eugénistes au Canada*, Montréal: L'Institut Familial, 1942.

Buckland, W. W., *A Manual of Roman Private Law*, 2. ed., Cambridge; The University Press, 1953.

Copleston, Frederick, *Contemporary Philosophy, Studies of Logical Positivism and Existentialism*, Westminster, Md.: The Newman Press, 1956.

Cronin, Michael, *The Science of Ethics*, 4. ed., 2 vols., Dublin: M. H. Gill and Son, Ltd., 1939.

De Lubac, Henri, *Sur les chemins de Dieu*, Aubier: Editions Montaigne, 1956.

Del Vecchio, Giorgio, *Philosophy of Law*, trans. from 8. ed. by Thomas Owen Martin, Washington, D. C.: The Catholic University of America Press, 1953.

D'Entrèves, A. P., *Natural Law, An Introduction to Legal Philosophy*, London: Hutchinson's University Library, 1951.

Denzinger, Henricus, *Enchiridion Symbòlorum, Definitionem et Declarationum de Rebus Fidei et Morum*, denuo compositum a Clemente Bannwart et curis iteratis editum a Ioanne Baptista Umberg, ed. 24-25., Barcelona: Editorial Herder, 1948.

Deploige, Simon, *Le conflit de la morale et de la sociologie*, 3. ed., Paris: Nouvelle Librairie Nationale, 1923.

Di Robilant, Enrico, *Significato del diritto naturale nell'ordinamento canonico*, Università de Torino, Memorie dell'Instituto giuridico, ser. 2, memoria 85, Torino: G. Giappichelli, 1954.

Dobzhansky, Theodosius, *Evolution, Genetics, and Man*, New York: John Wiley and Sons, Inc., London: Chapman and Hall, Ltd., 1955.

Farrell, Walter, *The Natural Moral Law According to St. Thomas and Suarez*, Ditchling: St. Dominic's Press, 1930.

Funk, Josephus, *De Jure Naturali Transcendente Jus Positivum*, Romae: Pontificia Universitas Gregoriana, 1947.

Garrigou-Lagrange, Réginald, *Christ the Savior*, trans. by Dom Bede Rose, St. Louis & London: B. Herder Book Co., 1950.

———, *God, His Existence and His Nature: A Thomistic Solution of Certain Agnostic Antinomies*, trans. from 5. ed. by Dom Bede Rose, St. Louis: B. Herder Book Co., 1934, 1936.

Gény, François, *Science et technique en droit privé positif*, 4 vols., Vol. I, 2. ed., 1922, Vol. II, 2. ed., 1927, Vol. III, 1921, Vol. IV, 2. ed., 1930, Paris: Recueil Sirey.

Gilson, Etienne, *Réalisme thomiste et critique de la connaissance*, Paris: Librairie Philosophique J. Vrin, 1947.

Graneris, Ioseph, *Philosophia Iuris*, Vol. I, *De Notione Iuris*, Torino: Società Editrice Internazionale, Romae: Libraria Pontificii Instituti Utriusque Iuris, 1943.

Gredt, Iosephus, *Elementa Philosophiae Aristotelico-Thomisticae*, 7. ed., 2 vols., Friburgi Brisgoviae: B. Herder & Co., 1937.

Ioannes Andreae, *In Titulum de Regulis Iuris Novella Commentaria*, Venetiis, 1581.

Jolowicz, H. F., *Historical Introduction to the Study of Roman Law*, 2. ed., Cambridge: The University Press, 1952.

Kreilkamp, Karl, *The Metaphysical Foundations of Thomistic Jurisprudence*, The Catholic University of America Philosophical Studies, Vol. 53, Washington, D. C.: The Catholic University of America Press, 1939.

Lachance, Louis, *Le Concept de Droit selon Aristote et saint Thomas*, Montréal: Albert Levesque; Paris: Recueil Sirey, 1933.

Lawson, F. H., *The Rational Strength of English Law*, London: Stevens & Sons, Ltd., 1951.

Leage, R. W., *Roman Private Law*, 2. ed., by C. H. Ziegler, London: Macmillan & Co., Ltd., Reprint, 1951.

Leclercq, Jacques, *Leçons de droit naturel*, 4 vols. in 5, Vol. I: *Le fondement du droit et de la société*, 3. éd., 1948, Vol. II: *L'Etat ou la politique*, 3. éd., 1948, Vol. III: *La famille*, 2. éd., 1945, Vol. IV: *Les droits et devoirs individuels*, P. I: *Vie, disposition de soi*, 2. éd., 1946, P. II: *Travail, propriété*, 2. éd., 1946, Namur: Ad. Wesmael-Charlier; Louvain: Société D'Etudes Morales, Sociales et Juridiques.

Lefebvre, Charles, *Les pouvoirs du juge en droit canonique, Contribution historique et doctrinale à l'étude du canon 20 sur la méthode et les sources en droit positif*, Paris: Recueil Sirey, 1938.

Lehane, Joseph, *The Morality of American Civil Legislation Concerning Eugenical Sterilization*, The Catholic University of America Studies in Sacred Theology, 1. series, n. 83, Washington, D. C.: The Catholic University of America Press, 1944.

Lohmuller, Martin N., *The Promulgation of Law*, The Catholic University of America Canon Law Studies, n. 241, Washington, D. C.: The Catholic University of America Press, 1947.

Lottin, Odon, *Le droit naturel chez saint Thomas D'Aquin et ses prédécesseurs*, 2. ed., Bruges, Belgique: Beyaert, 1931.

Maritain, Jacques, *A Preface to Metaphysics, Seven Lectures on Being*, New York: Sheed & Ward, 1948.

———, *Les Degrés du Savoir*, 5. ed., Paris: Desclée & Co., 1946.

———, *Les droits de l'homme et la loi naturelle*, Paris: Hartmann, 1947.

———, *Man and the State*, Chicago: The University of Chicago Press, 1951.

———, *Neuf leçons sur les notions premières de la philosophie morale*, Paris: Pierre Téqui, 1949.

———, *The Person and the Common Good*, London: Geoffrey Bles, 1948.

———, *The Rights of Man and Natural Law*, London: Geoffrey Bles, The Centenary Press, 1944.

Martin, Thomas Owen, *Adverse Possession, Prescription and Limitation of Actions, The Canonical "Praescriptio," A Commentary on Canon 1508*, The Catholic University of America Canon Law Studies, n. 202, Washington, D. C.: The Catholic University of America Press, 1944.

Messner, J., *Social Ethics*, trans. by J. J. Doherty, St. Louis & London: B. Herder Book Co., 1949.

Michiels, Gommarus, *Normae Generales Juris Canonici, Commentarius Libri I Codicis Juris Canonici*, 2 vols., ed. altera, Parisiis-Tornaci-Romae: Desclée et Socii, 1949.

———, *Principia Generalia de Personis in Ecclesia, Commentarius Libri II Codicis Juris Canonici, Canones Praeliminares*, 2. ed. penitus retractata et notabiliter aucta, Parisiis-Tornaci-Romae: Desclée et Socii, 1955.

Olgiati, Francesco, *Il Concetto di Giuridicità in San Tommaso d'Aquino*, 2. ed., Milano: Società Editrice "Vita e Pensiero," 1944.

Pegis, Antony, *Basic Writings of St. Thomas Aquinas*, New York: Random House, 1945.

Plato, *Statesman*, from *The Dialogues of Plato*, trans. by B. Jowett, 2 vols., 13. printing, New York: Random House, copyright 1937.

Reiffenstuel, Anacletus, *Jus Canonicum Universum complectens Tractatum de Regulis Juris*, Parisiis, 1864-1870.

Renard, Georges, *La théorie des* LEGES MERE POENALES, Paris: Recueil Sirey, 1929.

———, *La valeur de la loi*, Paris: Recueil Sirey, 1928.

———, *Le Droit, La Justice et la Volonté*, Paris: Recueil Sirey, 1924.

———, *Le Droit, l'Ordre et la Raison*, Paris: Recueil Sirey, 1927.

Riley, Lawrence Joseph, *The History, Nature and Use of EPIKEIA in Moral Theology*, The Catholic University of America Studies in Sacred Theology, 2. series, n. 17, Washington, D. C.: The Catholic University of America Press, 1948.

Roberti, Franciscus, *De Delictis et Poenis*, Vol. I, P. II, Romae: Libraria Pontificii Instituti Utriusque Iuris, 1938.

Rommen, Heinrich A., *The Natural Law, A Study in Legal and Social History and Philosophy*, trans. by Thomas R. Hanley, St. Louis: B. Herder Book Co., 1947.

Schmalzgrueber, Franciscus, *Jus Ecclesiasticum Universum brevi methodo ad discentium utilitatem explicatum seu lucubrationes canonicae in quinque libros decretalium Gregorii IX Pontificis Maximi*, Romae, 1843-1845.

Sertillanges, *La philosophie des lois*, Collection d'Essais "Faits et Idées," Vol. II, Paris: Editions Alsatia, 1946.

Suarez, Franciscus, *Opera Omnia*, ed. nova a Carolo Breton, Vols. V & VI: *Tractatus de Legibus et Legislatore Deo*, Parisiis, 1856.

———, *Tractatus de Legibus ac Deo Legislatore*, cura et studio Raphaelis Caccavo, Neapoli, 1872.

Thomas Aquinas, St., *Expositio super Librum Boethii de Trinitate*, ed. B. Decker, Leiden: Brill, 1955.

———, *Scriptum super Sententiis Magistri Petri Lombardi*, 4 vols., ed. M. F. Moos, Paris: P. Lethielleux, 1947.

———, *Summa contra Gentiles*, ed. Leonina Manualis, Romae: Desclée-Herder, 1934.

———, *Summa Theologiae*, cura et studio Instituti Studiorum Medievalium Ottaviensis ad textum S. Pii Papae V iussu confectum recognita, 2. ed. (Commissio Piana), 5 vols., Ottawa, Canada, 1953.

Van Hove, A., *De Legibus Ecclesiasticis, Commentarium Lovaniense in Codicem Iuris Canonici*, Vol. I, Tom. II, Mechliniae-Romae: Dessain, 1930.

Vermeersch, A., *Quaestiones de Justitia ad usum hodiernum scholastice disputatae*, Brugis: Beyaert, Romae & Ratisbonae: F. Pustet, Lutetiae Parisiorum: P. Lethielleux, 1901.

Webster's New Collegiate Dictionary, 2. ed., Springfield, Mass.: G & C. Merriam Co., 1956.

ARTICLES

Aubert, Jean-Marie, "Les citations de droit romain dans l'oeuvre de saint Thomas," *Revue de droit Canonique*, III (1953) 173-194, 317-335; IV (1954) 252-271; V (1955), 147-170.

Corwin, Edward S., "Natural Law and Constitutional Law," *University of Notre Dame Natural Law Institute Proceedings*, Indiana: College of Law, University of Notre Dame, III (1949), 47-81.

De Koninck, Charles, "General Standards and Particular Situations in Relation to the Natural Law," *Proceedings of the American Philosophical Association*, Washington, D. C.: The Catholic University of America, XXIV (1950), 28-32.

Kuttner, Stephan, "Natural Law and Canon Law," *University of Notre Dame Natural Law Institute Proceedings*, Indiana: College of Law, University of Notre Dame, III (1949), 83-116.

Laprat, R., "Prescription," *Dictionnaire de Théologie Catholique*, ed. A. Vacant, E. Mangenot, E. Amann, Paris: Letouzey et Ané, T. XIII (1936), col. 116-131.

Leclercq, Jacques, "*Note sur la position actuelle du droit naturel*," Revue néoscolastique de philosophie, XLI (1938), 267-278.

Lefebvre, Charles, "Epikie," *Dictionnaire de Droit Canonique*, Paris: Letouzey et Ané, V (1953), col. 364-375.

———, "Equité," *Dictionnaire de Droit Canonique*, Paris: Letouzey et Ané, V (1953), col. 394-410.

———, "Le rôle de l'équité en droit canonique," *Ephemerides Iuris Canonici*, VII (1951), 137-153.

Lottin, Odon, "La définition classique de la loi," *Revue néoscolastique de philosophie*, XXVII (1925), 131-145; 243-273.

North, Arthur A. - Ortiz, Pacifico, "A Return to the Natural Law," *Thought*, XXX (Winter, 1955-1956), 525-536.

O'Sullivan, Richard, "The Natural Law and Common Law," *University of Notre Dame Natural Law Institute Proceedings*, Indiana: College of Law, University of Notre Dame, III (1949), 9-44.

Phelan, Gerald, "Person and Liberty," *Proceedings of the American Catholic Philosophical Association, The Problem of Liberty*, Washington, D. C.: The Catholic University of America, XVI (1940), 53-69.

Simon, Yves, "Liberty and Authority," *Proceedings of the American Catholic Philosophical Association, The Problem of Liberty*, Washington, D. C.: The Catholic University of America, XVI (1940), 86-114.

Van Overbeke, P., "De Relatione Ordinem Iuridicum Inter et Ordinem Moralem," *Ephemerides Theologicae Lovanienses*, XI (1934), 289-346.

Wolff, Hans Julius, Review of *Das altrömische Ius*, Studien zur Rechtsgeschichte und Rechtsvorstellung der Römer von Max Kaser, "Notes and Reviews," *Seminar, Annual Extraordinary Number of The Jurist*, VII (1949), 86-95.

DICTIONARIES

Dictionnaire de Droit Canonique, ed. by A. Villien, E. Magnin, A. Amanieu, R. Naz, Paris: Letouzey et Ané, 1924—

Dictionnaire de Théologie Catholique, ed. by A. Vacant, E. Mangenot, E. Amann, Paris: Letouzey et Ané, 1903—

PERIODICALS

Ephemerides Iuris Canonici, Romae, 1945—

Ephemerides Theologicae Lovanienses, Louvain, 1924—

Revue de Droit Canonique, Strasbourg, 1951—

Revue Néoscolastique de Philosophie, Louvain, 1910-1946; *Revue Néoscolastique*, 1894-1909; *Revue Philosophique de Louvain*, 1947—

Seminar, Annual Extraordinary Number of The Jurist, Washington, 1943-1955.

Thought, New York, 1926—

PROCEEDINGS

Proceedings of the American Catholic Philosophical Association, Washington, 1926—

University of Notre Dame Natural Law Institute Proceedings, Indiana, 1947—

ALPHABETICAL INDEX

BIOGRAPHICAL NOTE

Raymond Francis Bégin was born in Lewiston, Maine, on February 19, 1928. He attended Saint Louis School of Auburn, Maine. From 1941 to 1946, he studied at Saint Charles Borromée Seminary, Sherbooke, P. Q., Canada. In September of 1946, he entered Saint Paul Seminary of the Catholic University of Ottawa, Canada. He received the degrees of Bachelor of Arts and Bachelor of Philosophy from Saint Paul Seminary in 1948. In 1952, he obtained the degree of Licentiate in Sacred Theology. He was ordained to the Priesthood on June 7, 1952, at the Cathedral of the Immaculate Conception, Portland, Maine.

After ordination he served in the parish of Saint John, Bangor, Maine, until November, 1953, when he was appointed to the parish of St. Agatha, St. Agatha, Maine. In September, 1955, he came to the School of Canon Law of the Catholic University of America, from which he received the degree of Bachelor of Canon Law in 1956, and the degree of Licentiate of Canon Law in 1957.

CANON LAW STUDIES*

392. Adams, Rev. Donald E., A.B., J.C.L., The truth required in the *preces* for rescripts.
393. Bégin, Rev. Raymond F., A.B., S.T.L., J.C.L., Natural law and positive law.
394. Clancy, Rev. Walter B., A.B., J.C.L., The rites and ceremonies of sacred ordination.
395. Cox, Rev. Ronald J., S.T.L., J.C.L., A study of the juridic status of laymen in the writing of the medieval canonists.
396. Demers, Rev. Francis L., O.M.I., A.B., J.C.L., Temporal administration of the religious house in a non-exempt clerical pontifical institute.
397. Dziadosz, Rev. Henry J., M.A., S.T.L., J.C.L., The provisions of the Decree "Spiritus Sancti munera": the law for the extraordinary minister of confirmation.
398. Gerhardt, Rev. Bernard C., A.B., S.T.L., J.C.L., Interpretation of rescripts.
399. Hackett, Rev. John H., A.B., J.C.L., The concept of public order.
400. Murphy, Rev. Richard J., O.M.I., S.T.L., J.C.L., The canonico-juridical status of a communist.
401. O'Connor, Rev. David, M.S.SS.T., J.C.L., Parochial relations and co-operation of the religious and secular clergy.

* For a complete list of the available numbers of this series apply to the Catholic University of America Press, 620 Michigan Avenue, N.E., Washington (17), D. C. for a general catalogue.

www.ingramcontent.com/pod-product-compliance
Lightning Source LLC
LaVergne TN
LVHW050235080826
844660LV00012B/532

9780813225531